John Lilburne:

Gentleman

Leveller

Quaker

Published by The Langley Press, 2020

John Lilburne:

Gentleman

Leveller

Quaker

by

Simon Webb

Contents

Mʳ Iohn Lilburn, a pious young Gentleman of about 22 or 23 yeares of age for suspition of printing & divulging certain of Dʳ Bastwickes & other bookes against Popish innovations, was censured in the Starr-Chamber to be whipt at a Carts-tayle from the fleet to Westminster, had therby about 200 lashes with a whip, was then presently upon it set one a pillorie, with a gagg in his mouth, was fined 500ˡⁱ and kept close prisoner in the fleet where day & night hee lay in iron shacles, and long time indured most barbarous and cruell usage.

I. Against Arizona

On March the thirteenth, 1963, one Ernesto Miranda was arrested in Arizona on suspicion of having kidnapped and raped an eighteen year-old girl some ten days earlier. After two hours of questioning by the Phoenix police, Mr Miranda signed a confession. We can imagine one of Ernesto's interrogators looking over his shoulder as he signed, thinking that this was now an open and shut case, and that Miranda's trial would be a mere formality. That was by no means how things turned out.

Ernesto Miranda was indeed found guilty as charged, and sentenced to twenty to thirty years in prison. But his attorney, Alvin Moore, lodged at appeal with the U.S. Supreme Court, which overturned the judgement passed down in Arizona. The Phoenix police, it seems, had not informed Ernesto that he had the right to a lawyer, and they had also neglected to remind him that, thanks to the celebrated Fifth Amendment, he also had the right to remain silent. The Supreme Court sent Mr Miranda back to Arizona to be tried again using better evidence.

Following the Supreme Court's ruling in the Miranda case, police in the U.S. started reading so-called 'Miranda warnings' to suspects, and incorporating the signing of 'Miranda cards' into the processing of people they arrested. These were supposed to ensure that suspects had indeed been advised of their rights. After his release in 1972, Ernesto Miranda made a modest living signing these cards for local police officers, who were required to carry them when on duty. Viewers of U.S. cop series on TV will have heard these rights, which actors playing arresting officers have to memorise along with the rest of their lines. The wording has varied over time, and it is different in different jurisdictions, but it is generally designed to inform suspects (who should already have been told that they are under arrest, and why) that they have the right to remain silent, but that anything they do say may be used in evidence against them; that they have the right to an attorney, etc.

One of the surprising aspects of the original Miranda case is that, writing about the Supreme Court's majority decision in favour of Miranda, Chief Justice Earl Warren referred to a case tried in London over three hundred years earlier. Warren mentioned the case of John Lilburne to show his readers how the fight for the rights of suspects under arrest was rooted deep in history.

Earl Warren's mention of John Lilburne probably led to some puzzled head-scratching on both sides of the Atlantic, even among historians, despite the fact that two excellent biographies of the man had been published during the twentieth century. Many of Lilburne's contemporaries would have been astonished to learn that his name had fallen into obscurity in this way, even after three hundred years. They would have counted him among a handful of the most famous, influential and even dangerous people of the middle of the seventeenth century in England. To many of his compatriots, Lilburne was 'Free-born John', the bold man who spoke truth to power without fear, and counted nobody superior to himself. To Earl Warren, the cases of both Lilburne and Miranda had to do with 'the privilege against self-incrimination'. Like Earl Warren himself, John Lilburne was concerned with other rights as well.

To pursue what he described as his duty, Lilburne was prepared to undergo years of imprisonment, brutal corporal punishment, severe poverty, exile and more. Perhaps he should be remembered in our century because still, all over the world, people are enduring the same privations and for the same causes. In the north of England, John Lilburne, gentleman, Leveller and Quaker, should be remembered as one of County Durham's most notable sons.

II. The Man from Thickley Punchardon

Older editions of the British Dictionary of National Biography insist that John Lilburne was born, around 1614, at Greenwich. Other sources assumed he had been born on the family estate in County Durham; and there was even an old northern tradition that he somehow managed to be born in Westminster Hall. Today the scholarly consensus is that John Lilburne was born in Sunderland, nearly three hundred miles away from London, on the North Sea coast of England: nobody seems to be certain exactly *when* he was born.

The family did have connections to Greenwich, where Thomas Hixon, John's maternal grandfather, had served as part of the court of the unfortunate King Charles I. There John Lilburne lived with his grandparents from the age of two to the age of six, before being brought back north to the family's modest estate at Thickley Punchardon (also called East Thickley) near Bishop Auckland in County Durham. Lilburne went to school at Bishop Auckland, and also attended the Royal Grammar School at Newcastle-upon-Tyne. He was never instructed at a university or an inn of court, and though he knew a little Latin, he is thought to have known no Greek at all. This would hardly be a disability to a twenty-first century individual with pretensions to learning, but in the seventeenth century many regarded a sound knowledge of Latin and Greek as the foundations of a good education.

In his 1649 pamphlet *Legal Fundamental Liberties of the People of England Revived*, Lilburne tells us that as a young apprentice in London he was able to supplement his education by reading:

the Bible, the Book of Martyrs, Luther's, Calvin's, Beza's, Cartwright's, Perkins', Molin's, Burton's, and Rogers' works, with multitude of other such like books that I had bought with my own money . . .

As we shall see, Lilburne was later influenced by his reading in the works of the celebrated jurist, Sir Edward Coke (pronounced 'Cook', 1552-1634). Strange to say, we actually have a picture of John Lilburne reading, or at least reading from, the *Institutions*, one of Coke's most important works. This picture is the engraving used as the frontispiece for a printed account of Lilburne's trial for treason in 1649. It shows John standing at the bar of the court, set up in the Guildhall in London, with the book in his hand.

According to Conyers Surtees' 1923 *History of New Shildon and East Thickley*, Thickley Punchardon got the second part of its name from one Hugh de Pountchardon, who was given the estate by Antony Bek, a bishop of Durham who died in 1311. Hugh himself seems to have got his surname from a place called Pontchardon in Normandy, and it is likely that he was a descendant of one of the Normans who came over to England at the time of the Conquest. Bek and Hugh feature in a little-known ghost story that Surtees re-tells in his 1923 book. Hugh is supposed to have died before the bishop, but de Pountchardon appeared to Bek while he was out hunting one day (although only the bishop could see him at that time). When the bishop, Hamlet-like, tried to question the ghost, Hugh hoisted up his shirt to show a set of cadaverous ribs, innocent of either skin or muscle.

'Old Thickley' was recorded in the Boldon Book, compiled on the orders of Hugh du Puiset, an earlier bishop of Durham, in 1183. The fact that Bishop Bek was granting lands to people, lands that had been recorded in a survey commissioned by a previous bishop, reflects the curious status of County Durham within England at this time, and for a long time afterwards. Historians have to refer to the Boldon Book to find out about Durham in the twelfth century because the county was not included in the Domesday Book, the much larger survey commissioned by

William the Conqueror a century earlier. As a steward of Bishop Anthony Bek once said:

There are two kings in England, namely the Lord King of England, wearing a crown in sign of his regality and the Lord Bishop of Durham wearing a mitre in place of a crown, in sign of his regality in the diocese of Durham.

Until 1836, the bishops of Durham were 'prince bishops', enjoying vast wealth and unique powers, and people of John Lilburne's generation tended to refer to what we now call County Durham as 'Bishopric'. The county has shrunk considerably since William van Mildert was the last prince bishop: because it still included Sunderland in the seventeenth century, we can say that John Lilburne was Durham born and bred.

The estate at Thickley Punchardon passed into the hands of a younger son of the Lilburne family in 1450: the Lilburnes held on to it until 1717, when it was sold to a Mr Thomas Gower. Surtees (who assumed that John Lilburne was born at Thickley) managed to trace the family back to the thirteenth century, but it may have originated in the Northumberland village of Lilburn before the Conquest. In his book *Sunderland Notables*, published in 1894, William Brockie tells us about a John Lilburne who was in possession of the Lilburn estate in Northumberland under King Edward II (died 1327) and a Sir John Lilburn who was there in the days of Edward III (died 1377). This Lilburn knight 'had the misfortune to be twice taken prisoner by the Scots,' once after a battle near Carham, and later after the battle of Otterburn in 1388. Brockie tells us that a Thomas Lilburne, his descendant, represented Northumberland in Parliament in 1434. The author of the *History of New Shildon and East Thickley* points out that a John Lilburne was Constable of Alnwick in the time of Henry VI, and that a Bartholomew Lilburne was with Henry VIII at the French port of Boulogne, probably in 1544 when the English were trying to capture the town. As we already know, our John Lilburne's mother Margaret was a daughter of Thomas Hixon, an official of the royal court of King Charles I at Greenwich.

11

A story told about Richard, John Lilburne's father, is sometimes taken as evidence that the Lilburnes of Thickley were constitutionally hot-tempered and violent. As related by Conyers Surtees, however, the tale loses much of its shock value. In 1638 the old man became embroiled in a dispute over the ownership of some land with his brother-in-law Ralph Claxton. Both proposed that the matter should be settled by trial by combat, which was still possible in English law at this time: the Lilburne/Claxton case was, however, the last during which the parties requested this form of decision-making.

His request for trial by combat does not, however, mean that Richard, then in his fifties, turned up at court with a freshly-sharpened sword, ready to fight. In fact both men turned up with champions hired to fight for them: George Cheney was Claxton's champion; Lilburne's was called William Peverel. And at no point were swords to be involved: George and William were to fight with sandbags attached to staffs. In the end, the fight never happened: it was delayed by various means until the law was changed so that legal cases could no longer be decided in this way. This meant that John Lilburne's father Richard won his case by default.

In keeping with the Lilburne family's distinguished history, John's older brother Robert, like John himself, played a major part during the political upheavals that were to plague Britain in the middle of the seventeenth century. He was a colonel in the Parliamentary army, and became one of the 'regicides' who signed the death-warrant of King Charles I. He was also involved in Oliver Cromwell's doomed attempt to found a university at Durham. During the Interregnum, Robert was a Member of Parliament for County Durham, and then represented the East Riding of Yorkshire. When Oliver Cromwell tried to divide up the administration of England between his unpopular major-generals, Robert Lilburne became part of that system.

During part of the Civil War, Robert's lieutenant-colonel was his own brother Henry, who was younger than both Robert and John. Henry was put in charge of Tynemouth Castle, the remains of which, with those of Tynemouth Priory, still dominate a rocky headland that looms over the North Sea at Tynemouth. In 1648 Henry unexpectedly switched sides and became a Royalist. In a chapter on the Durham Lilburnes in David Marcome's book *The Last Principality*, William Dumble suggests that Henry was seduced over to the king's side by the Royalist prisoners who were then being held in the castle. One characteristic of Henry's older brother John was that he was able to discourse with, and even make valuable friends of, people who disagreed with him, but without altering his own opinions.

The commander who quickly re-captured Tynemouth Castle for the Parliamentary side at this time was Arthur Haselrig, with whom John Lilburne was to have extensive dealings later. Haselrig remarked that Henry Liburne 'did not give the least suspicion of being a traitor . . . till the day of his revolt'. Poor Henry was killed during Haselrig's siege.

In the generation above the three Lilburne brothers Robert, John and Henry, George Lilburne, their father's younger brother, was an important merchant with an impressive house in Sunderland. He was so dominant in the politics of the place that he was described as 'Lilburne the great factotum of Sunderland that rules both the religion and wealth of the town'. At times, George formed a formidable part of the Puritan, middle-class opposition to the prince bishops' domination of the spiritual, political, legal and commercial life of County Durham. In 1641, for instance, he contributed to a petition sent to London to complain about the ideas and behaviour of the Bishop of Durham and his followers, who were adherents of the 'high-church', 'Arminian' style of churchmanship then associated with the king and William Laud, the Archbishop of Canterbury. In 1641 Laud was imprisoned by Parliament, and the Bishop of Durham in 1641, Thomas Morton, was forced to step down when Parliament abolished bishops in 1647. Later, George Lilburne would contribute to another petition, calling for the captured King Charles I to be put on trial.

It is likely that John Lilburne's uncle George was better-off than his older brother, John's father, who inherited the estate at Thickley Punchardon. Richard would have been relying on land for much of his income; and in her 1961 biography of John

Lilburne, Pauline Gregg pointed out that agriculture in the north of England was in a bad way in the seventeenth century. In the best of times, temperatures up here are lower than they are in the lush fields of the Home Counties, and the growing-season is shorter. High winds, torrential rain, hail, snow and untimely frosts can devastate crops. In the seventeenth century, plague, clashes with the Scots, bad harvests and the resulting famines depopulated the land, and many of the people who were left on it had nowhere to live and nothing to eat. Perhaps as little as two percent of usable land was actually being cultivated, and throughout the country during John Lilburne's entire adult life bad harvests outnumbered good ones. The difficulty of making a decent living out of estates such as the Lilburnes' at Thickley Punchardon may explain why John's father Richard spent so much time at court in London.

John Lilburne, future leader of the Levellers, never forgot his roots among the minor provincial gentry. Although it is possible to identify him as a working-class hero, the man himself was always insistent on his aristocratic background and his status as a gentleman. In his 1638 pamphlet *A Work of the Beast*, he called himself 'the son of a gentleman', and added that his friends were 'of rank and quality in the country where they live'. Perhaps we should call Lilburne a hero *of* the people, though he did not come *from* the people.

III. Against the Bishops

Although he always insisted on his status as a gentleman, John Lilburne, as we have seen, was the second son of a minor gentry family based in a part of England where the income to be made from land, manufactures and the famous Durham coal-mines was not enough to allow the Lilburne sons to live lives of leisure. One suspects that even if John had been given a lucrative estate of his own at an early age, his active spirit would not have allowed him to remain on it for very long, planting turnips and laying out ornamental gardens.

In 1630, when he was perhaps sixteen years old, Richard Lilburne's second son was packed off to London, where he was apprenticed to a cloth-merchant called Thomas Hewson. Today the word 'apprenticeship' is usually applied to training in some manual occupation. In modern terms, Lilburne's apprenticeship with a wholesale clothier in Candlewick Street (now Cannon Street) was probably more like a paid internship in the offices of a successful businessman than time served, for example, in a humble shoemaker's workshop. In the twenty-first century, such opportunities are often arranged through the useful contacts of well-set-up parents: according to Pauline Gregg's biography of Lilburne, Hewson the clothier may have been connected to John's mother's family, the Hixons. Certainly he was a County Durham man, from the ancient village of Aycliffe, and regularly employed apprentices from his home county. Aycliffe is just over thirteen miles south of Durham City, and a few miles south-east of Bishop Auckland.

If there was a Hixon-Hewson-Lilburne family connection, then this might explain why Hewson was prepared to overlook a surprising legal attack launched on him by his young apprentice just a few years after John had joined the business. It seems that Hewson was in the habit of verbally abusing his apprentice, and so young John complained about this to the Lord Chamberlain. One might have thought that this would have caused a permanent rift between master and apprentice, but Hewson became an early example of a man who was attacked by John Lilburne, but continued to help and respect him. In later years, these 'forgivers' of Lilburne included Oliver Cromwell himself, and the aforementioned Arthur Haslerig, a powerful man in the north during the Interregnum.

In his *Legal Fundamental Liberties* Lilburne explained how it was while he was apprenticed to Hewson that he found time to read books on religious, political and philosophical subjects that he had bought for himself. In this pamphlet, which includes a lot of fascinating autobiographical material, the northerner explains that 'several days in the week I had spare time enough': he implies that this was because the core of Hewson's business was a warehouse. This evokes an image of the young apprentice propped up on bolts of cloth, his nose deep inside some weighty tome.

Thomas Hewson, Lilburne's master, was a Puritan: a whole book could be written about what the word 'Puritan' meant at this time, but the most relevant points in this context are that the Puritans opposed elaborate church services, and favoured a flatter, more democratic way of organising the Church. The Church, in its many forms, was of course far more important to far more people in the middle of the seventeenth century in England than it is to most people now, and religion and politics were so tightly bound together in those days that they were quite inextricable.

Puritans like Thomas Hewson and some of his London associates were dissatisfied with the state of the Church of England as it was under King Charles I. Charles was, like all English monarchs since Henry VIII, the head of the Church. Many of Charles's Protestant subjects harboured a deep suspicion of the Roman Catholic Church, which had once been such a powerful force in England, and continued to hold sway in much of continental Europe. To many Puritans, a sign that the Church of England might be more Roman Catholic than was good for it was the retention of bishops in its hierarchy. A leading member of the London Puritan underground at the time was the writer and physician John Bastwick, who was locked up in the Gatehouse prison in Westminster because of his writings against the bishops. It seems that John Lilburne learned a great deal from his visits to this man, who later became one of his enemies. Not all of Bastwick's teaching was about Puritan doctrine: in his book *A Just Defence of John Bastwick* (1645), Bastwick himself says of Lilburne that:

When he first became my scholar, though he were honest and religious, yet he was but a mere country courtier, and very rough hewn; so that he could neither make a leg with grace nor put off his hat seemly, till I had polished him and taught him all his postures of courtship, and now he is become a very gallant fellow. I have made him fit for all gentlemen's and noblemen's society.

Lilburne came to resent Bastwick's implication that without his help he would have been 'buried in obscurity', and in his *Innocency and Truth Justified* (also 1645) he insisted that his education in the north had been 'the best which the country afforded'.

Lilburne's visits to the Gatehouse were noted by the authorities, and they became very suspicious when John made a visit to the Netherlands, where they knew the writings of Bastwick and other controversial British authors were being printed, and from where they were being imported into England.

At the time, books were censored via a licensing scheme, and unlicensed texts were regarded as illegal. The licensing was overseen by the Stationer's Company, in effect a craft guild for printers, which the government was happy to use as an agency for tracking down offending works and authors, and seizing unlicensed printing presses. It was therefore pursuivants employed by the Stationers who seized John Lilburne in a narrow London alley in December 1637, shortly after his return from the Low

Countries.

According to his own account in a pamphlet called *The Christian Man's Trial*, published in 1641, the pursuivants, two of whom were 'great fellows', were very rough with him, and tried to bind him with his own cloak so that he could not draw his sword. Eventually they threw their prisoner over a sugar-chest so as to get his sword off him. After a night at the house of one of the pursuivants, Lilburne was kept at the Gatehouse and then at the Fleet prison. From there he was taken, on the fourteenth of January, to be questioned by Sir John Banks, the Attorney General. This was the beginning of the case that was cited by U.S. Chief Justice Earl Warren in his statement following the Miranda case over three hundred years later.

Banks tried something like the 'good cop' strategy so well known to viewers of modern TV detective series, although there were no English police at the time, and there seems not to have been a 'bad cop' present. Lilburne tells us that in true good cop style, Banks 'at our first coming together, he did kindly intreat [treat] me; and made me sit down by him, and put on my hat'. The Attorney General then tried to seduce his young guest into incriminating himself by asking him a series of questions about his activities in the Netherlands: Where were you there? What books did you see in Holland? Who printed all these books? Did you not send over some of these books?

At this point, Lilburne had not been charged (as we would say now) with any specific crime, and had not been properly acquainted with any of the evidence which had led to his arrest. Despite his youth, his lack of experience of the law, and the exalted position of the Attorney General, he still had the presence of mind to protest:

I am not willing to answer you to any more of these questions because I see you go about by this examination to ensnare me, for seeing the things for which I am imprisoned cannot be proved against me, you would get other matter out of my examination, and therefore if you will not ask me about the thing laid to my charge, I shall answer no more . . .

'About ten or twelve days after' Lilburne was supposed to be being taken to Gray's Inn, but found himself at the office of the Star Chamber, a court of law that was then notorious as a pseudo-legal instrument of official cruelty and oppression. The term 'Star Chamber' is still regularly used to describe atrocious show-trials or any other legal procedure that is grossly unfair. Not surprisingly, the Star-Chamber was abolished by Parliament in 1641, partly because of the treatment Lilburne received there.

In the Star Chamber office the officials tried to make Lilburne swear an oath and enter his name, and even tried to make him pay for the privilege. This he refused to do, as he considered such an oath illegal. As Andrew Sharp points out in the current Dictionary of National Biography article on Lilburne, the so-called 'ex-officio' oath the Star Chamber officials were trying to make Lilburne swear to was not in fact illegal at the time, but it may have been enough for John that the jurist Sir Edward Coke had condemned such oaths in his writings. Not surprisingly, the personnel in the Star Chamber office began to stare in amazement at this young northerner who dared to question the legal basis of their ancient institution: they were used to getting their own way.

John Lilburne still refused to be sworn in when he appeared before the Star Chamber itself, though William Laud, the Archbishop of Canterbury himself, demanded that he do so (in his own account of this trial, Lilburne refers to Laud as 'the Arch Prelate'). It is interesting that Laud, who would be executed by Parliament in 1645, should have ordered Lilburne to take the oath, even though the archbishop must have known that the prisoner had already been asked to do so by the court officials. It may be that Laud thought that his status as Archbishop of Canterbury would convince Lilburne, even over-awe him, into compliance. As the northerner's subsequent career would prove, he was not one to be over-awed by anyone.

The Star Chamber tried Lilburne together with an octogenarian called John Wharton, an inveterate publisher of illegal books and a friend of John Bastwick's. During the proceedings, Laud said that Lilburne 'hath been one of the notoriousest dispersers of libellous books that is in the kingdom'. Pointing at Wharton, Laud added, 'and that is the Father of them all'.

The venerable father of the dispersers of libellous books was not given time to speak his whole mind in court, but he gave the warden of the Fleet prison a taste of it after he and Lilburne had been sentenced. According to Lilburne's *Christian Man's Trial*, Wharton:

told the warden, how the bishops were the greatest tyrants that ever were since Adam's creation; and that they were more crueller than the cannibals, those men-eaters, for (said he) they presently [quickly] devoured men, and put an end to their pain, but the bishops do it by degrees, and are many years in exercising their cruelty and tyranny upon those that stand out against them; and therefore are worse than the very cannibals . . .

Because of his great age, Wharton was only fined, imprisoned and forced to stand in the pillory. Lilburne's punishment was far more severe. On the eighteenth of April 1638 he was stripped to the waist, tied to the back of a cart and whipped with knotted cords all the way to the pillory. Before he started whipping Lilburne, the executioner said to him, 'I have whipped many a rogue but now I shall whip an honest man. But be not discouraged, it will be soon over'. The prisoner's route was lined with supporters, who asked him how he was, encouraged him to bear his suffering cheerfully, and prayed for him.

The sun was unusually strong for an April day in London, but Lilburne was denied the use of his hat. When he was finally put in the pillory, John found that he still had strength to launch into a lengthy speech, which included biblical quotations, arguments against the bishops of the Church of England, autobiographical details and assertions of his own innocence. At last the Warden of the Fleet prison appeared with a 'fat lawyer' and commanded Lilburne to shut up. When he refused to do so, they gagged him, but he distributed forbidden literature from his pockets, then stamped his feet.

IV. Against the King

Lilburne's 'censure', as his punishment was called, the brave manner in which he faced it, and the daring speech he had given from the pillory, made the northerner an instant celebrity in London. His own account of that day, in his pamphlet *A Work of the Beast*, secured his reputation, particularly among those who were already opposed to the power of the bishops and the perceived illegitimacy of the royal government.

The year 1638, when Lilburne was so cruelly 'censured', was one of the eleven years of Charles I's personal rule, also known as 'the eleven years' tyranny', when his majesty attempted to run the country without a parliament. Since only Parliament could impose taxes, the king tried various means to raise money, including the notorious 'ship money', the raising of which fell within the royal prerogative.

Ship money was traditionally levied in coastal areas, and the funds were supposed to go to the building of ships in time of war. As such Sunderland, John Lilburne's probable birth-place, was liable to pay the king's ship-money, and at first the good citizens of the town could hardly avoid it. Thomas Morton, who was bishop of Durham from 1632, granted Sunderland an enhanced level of independence in a charter of 1634. Under the new charter, the town was to be governed by a mayor and twelve aldermen. Our friend George Lilburne, John's uncle, was one of the original twelve, and was even mayor when his poor nephew was being flogged down in London. It would have been difficult for Sunderland to have avoided paying ship money in 1634 when it was re-introduced, because that was when their new charter was granted, and the first mayor, Sir William Bellasis, was the official collector of the ancient tax in County Durham.

Sunderland paid its ship money in full in 1634 and 1635, but after that the town resisted, as did many others. It is no surprise that George Lilburne, from the Puritan Durham family, played a major part in the resistance. George's stance was not limited to his objection to ship money, however. When the First Civil War broke out in 1642, George and his associates objected to King Charles's Commission of Array, whereby that monarch hoped to inspire Royalist bigwigs all over the country to muster troops. George's stance set him against William Cavendish, First Earl of Newcastle, whom Charles had put in charge of the northern counties. The Royalists threw George into prison at Durham, then forced him to march over seventy miles 'through mire and dirt' to York, 'where they threw him in a dungeon and used him barbarously 14 months', despite the fact that he was sixty years old at the beginning of his ordeal.

In their 2007 history of Sunderland Maureen Meikle and Christine Newman suggest that political and religious ideas may have fed into Sunderland's decision not to line the pockets of the king. The locals may have been influenced not only by the old-style Puritanism of families like the Lilburnes, but also by the new ideas of London radicals like John Lilburne, perhaps transmitted via forbidden pamphlets smuggled aboard ships plying the east coast routes between the river Wear and the Thames.

After his punishment in April 1638, Lilburne remained in the Fleet prison until November 1640. In the same month, King Charles was obliged to recall Parliament when a Scottish army invaded England. During the first week of what became known as the Long Parliament, the Member for Cambridge pressed for Lilburne's release. The name of this MP was Oliver Cromwell.

Thanks to Cromwell's efforts and Lilburne's status as a *cause célèbre*, the northerner was released from the Fleet. Like many ex-convicts, he then had to face the question of what he was to do next. It seems there was no question of his returning to his employment at Hewson's, or of his setting up on his own as a clothier, the trade he is supposed to have learned from his old master. His wealthy uncle George, the 'factotum' of Sunderland, sent down enough money to set his nephew up as a brewer; and in 1641 John married Elizabeth, the daughter of a London merchant called Henry Dewell.

In May 1641 the House of Commons declared that Lilburne's punishment in 1638 and his subsequent imprisonment had been 'bloody, wicked, cruel, barbarous, and tyrannical'. They awarded him financial payments as recompense, but as was to happen again in John's life, he never seems to have seen the money.

Unfortunately the newly-wed, recently released from prison, and with a new business to get up and running, could not settle down to the comfortable life of a London brewer. During the month when the House of Commons exonerated Lilburne, the capital was gripped by the attempts of the same House to bring down 'Black Tom Tyrant', alias Thomas Wentworth, Earl of Strafford. His enemies saw Strafford as a very dangerous and powerful ally of the king, who might lead armies, raised in Yorkshire and Ireland, against Parliament itself.

Great pressure was put on the 'Straffordians', Strafford's followers, by the hysterical crowds that flocked to Westminster, baying for Black Tom's blood. Lilburne was in the thick of the disturbances, and got into trouble for crying out that if Strafford was not brought to justice, 'they would pull the king out of Whitehall'. For this he was arrested, but his case was brought before the House of Lords on the very day that the Commons declared his previous punishment wicked and tyrannical, and the charges could not be made to stick. A few days later, there was more trouble when Lilburne attended Strafford's execution; and in December of the same year he received a musket-wound during a protest against the power of the bishops.

In January 1642 King Charles I left London with a small group of some thirty or forty followers, his plan being to raise some sort of an army to fight the parliament that seemed unable to reconcile itself to his ideas; and had even executed his supporter 'Black Tom' Strafford in May of the previous year. Also in 1641, Parliament had imprisoned William Laud, the archbishop of

Canterbury and Charles's great ally, in the Tower of London. This was the same 'Arch Prelate' who had taken such a high-handed attitude with John Lilburne during his trial in the Star Chamber in 1638.

Parliament needed to raise an army, and John Lilburne signed up in the summer of 1642. He became a captain of foot in Lord Brooke's troop, and fought at the battle of Edgehill in Warwickshire, in October 1642. Edgehill was indecisive, but the smaller battle at Brentford to the west of London was a victory for the Royalist troops, in this case led by King Charles's nephew Prince Rupert, who was then only twenty-three years old. At Brentford, Rupert captured about five hundred prisoners, among them John Lilburne. John was taken to Oxford, then the Royalist headquarters, and when he refused to defect to Charles's side, he was tried for treason. His family pride asserted itself again when he insisted that he would not answer to his indictment if it called him a 'yeoman', since his family 'were gentlemen, and had continued ever since William the Conqueror in the bishopric of Durham'.

There was a strong chance that Lilburne would be executed for treason at Oxford, but the Parliamentarian authorities in London had been persuaded, by Lilburne's wife, that they should threaten to kill one of their Royalist prisoners for every one of their own men executed at Oxford. Usually the least interesting part of such a story would be the name of the messenger who brought the news that Lilburne and his comrades were to be freed, from London to Oxford. In this case, the identity of that brave messenger is particularly interesting – it was Lilburne's wife Elizabeth, who brought the good news across sixty miles of war-torn England, though she was pregnant at the time.

When he returned to London, John learned that Elizabeth had not only petitioned for his release and brought the relevant document to Oxford herself: she had also managed to secure him a government job that would bring in about a thousand pounds a year.

Such an income, amounting to over two thousand pounds a week in modern money, would have been extremely useful to the

Lilburnes at this time: John had just sold his brewery at a loss, and there seems to have been no prospect of another civilian job for him. But the northerner rejected the lucrative offer of employment and returned to the army, saying that he would rather fight for eight pence a day till he saw 'the liberties and peace of England settled'.

Lilburne returned to the war as a major in Colonel Edward King's regiment, a position given to him by Cromwell himself, who was great friends with John at the time. Oliver wanted Lilburne to report back to him if his colonel 'should break out to the dishonour of my engagement and the detriment of the public'. As Cromwell's spy in the camp, Lilburne soon had plenty to report. Edward King turned out to be cowardly, incompetent and corrupt, and Lilburne did not hesitate to report this to Cromwell. As a reward, Oliver promoted Lilburne to the rank of Lieutenant-Colonel in the regiment of dragoons commanded by Edward Montagu, second earl of Manchester. It was under Manchester that Lilburne fought at the battle of Marston Moor, west of York, in July 1644, which proved to be a famous victory for the Parliamentary side.

Manchester had been an effective soldier earlier in the war, but shortly after the slaughter of Marston Moor he seems to have lost his nerve and become timid, inactive and reclusive, missing opportunities to beat the Cavaliers. He now believed that the war could not be won for his side, and said of the king that, 'If we fight a hundred times and beat him ninety-nine he will be king still, but if he beats us but once, or the last time, we shall be hanged, we shall lose our estates, and our posterities be undone'.

It is hardly surprising that restless John Lilburne could not easily work under Manchester in his new, hesitant, time-wasting mood, and the two clashed when Lilburne managed to capture Tickhill Castle in Yorkshire, without any bloodshed, in July 1644. On hearing this news, which should have been music to his ears, Manchester publicly called Lilburne a 'rogue, rascal and base fellow', remarked that the army 'was much troubled with such busy rogues' and added that his victorious Lieutenant-Colonel 'deserved to be hanged'.

This marked the end of John Lilburne's military career. He said that Manchester's words 'did so vex and perplex my very soul' that he could 'never from that day . . . draw my sword, nor engage my life in the way of a soldier with that freeness, alacrity and cheerfulness as formerly I had done.'

V. Paper War

Given his family's deep-seated Puritanism, his outspoken hostility to the bishops, his residence in London (a Puritan stronghold) and the treatment he had received during the period of the king's personal rule, it was perhaps inevitable that Lilburne should have joined the Parliamentary forces in 1642, rather than those of the Royalists. In the autobiographical part of his *Legal Fundamental Liberties*, Lilburne reminds the reader that he had, after all, 'smarted under the king's irregular government'.

It seems, however, that Lilburne did reflect for a while on his decision before he acted on it by becoming a 'Roundhead'. The knowledge of the law that he had acquired convinced him that the laws of England justified the power of the king; but as usual his attitude to these laws was influenced by the ideas of Edward Coke. According to Lilburne, Coke believed that laws could be challenged if they ceased to be reasonable. 'Where reason ceaseth, there the law ceaseth', Lilburne writes, and he implies that the hated ship-money was an example of the 'absurdities and inconveniences' that ordinary citizens should not have to tolerate from any ruler. For Lilburne, the relationship between king and subject was like a 'compact . . . betwixt two parties . . . to bind both equally alike, king as well as people'. He hints that by 1642 he felt that the king had broken his side of the compact 'in twenty particulars, as by ship-money, projects, etc'.

Thanks to Coke, whom he describes as 'that most excellent of English lawyers', Lilburne was able to satisfy himself that Parliament's rebellion against the king was legal. He also tells us that he was drawn to the Parliamentary side by Parliament's:

> . . . words and declarations, which were to secure the people's laws and liberties to them, and not in the least to seek themselves; to provide for their weal, but not for their woe . . .

Lilburn's attitude to Parliament's words and declarations was turned upside-down as he became disillusioned with both Parliament and his commanding officers toward the end of his military service. Now no longer fighting the 'unreasonable' king with sword and matchlock rifle, Lilburne turned to fighting Parliament with pen and printing-press.

As we know, Lilburne's pamphlet *A Work of the Beast* was his description of the barbaric 'censure' he had suffered in the spring of 1638. With this work, and with *The Christian Man's Trial*, his account of the legal abuses that had got him to the pillory, published in 1641, Lilburne had entered the 'paper war' of pamphlets which was such a characteristic feature of political life at this time. Despite the government's censorship, enforced by the Stationer's Company in league with the Star Chamber, controversial tracts and pamphlets poured out of carefully concealed unlicensed presses. When the Star Chamber was abolished, similar mechanisms were created to fill its role as draconian suppressor of printed ideas; but the stream of inflammatory pamphlets still flowed.

At the heart of establishment control of the printing trade was the monopoly enjoyed by the Stationer's Company, which as we know went to great lengths to prevent anyone from infringing their rights. As tends to happen with monopolies, the lack of competition meant that the privileged Stationers grew sloppy, allowed their professional standards to decline, and became too insular to embrace technological improvements, many of which originated on the Continent.

If the work of the 'official' printers was poor, the products of the illegal presses could be appalling. As Colin Clair says in his 1965 *History of Printing in Britain*, the controversial pamphlets of the Civil War and Interregnum were often 'in workmanship slipshod, in typography vile, dressed up with ancient blocks and printed on the poorest of paper'. As a result, students of the controversies of the period are often forced to sweat through facsimiles of texts in which many words are so blurred and/or meanly inked that they can only be guessed at.

The 'ancient blocks' Clair refers to were wooden blocks bearing woodcuts or wood engravings, many of which would have been crude to start with, and may have become damaged or worn-out over the years. These would nevertheless still be used to 'dress up' printed books and pamphlets, although the images might have been quite irrelevant to the printed text.

An alternative to wooden blocks were engraved metal plates that, in skilled hands, yielded a subtler and more detailed image. Thanks to this technology, we have two fairly authoritative portraits of John Lilburne, one from 1640, engraved by George Glover, and an anonymous engraving from 1649. All subsequent portraits look as if they were based on one of these, including one by the celebrated Wenceslaus Hollar, who was born in Prague in 1607. The two most authoritative engravings of John Lilburne both show a young man with dark curly hair and a moustache. There is no trace of a beard in 1640, but by 1649 a dark triangular 'tip' has appeared below the bottom lip. In 1640 the hair is worn short and the curls cluster round the ears – by 1649 it is just brushing the shoulders.

To judge by the 1649 portrait, Lilburne's locks had recovered from the infection that had rendered him bald during his imprisonment at Oxford. This was probably caused by typhus or 'prison fever', spread by human body-lice. This was such a threat to public health that when the Old Bailey Courthouse, where Lilburne was to be tried in 1653, was rebuilt after the Great Fire of 1666, the builders deliberately missed out a wall, leaving the building open to the elements. It was hoped that the fresh air thus admitted would clean out the poisonous 'miasma' by which fevers were thought to spread.

Both the 1640 and 1649 engravings of John Lilburne show a well-dressed man, with immaculate lace collars and, in the full-length 1649 version, slashed breeches with tassels and elaborate boots. From the artistic point of view, Glover's head-and-shoulders portrait is good plain work, but the later picture has a stiff, unnatural posture: the subject looks as if he is about to topple backwards.

Hollar's engraving, which must be based on Glover's, is more subtle and expressive; but it is to be regretted that John Lilburne never sat for one of the great portraitists of the age, such as Anthony Van Dyck or Peter Lely. John's older brother Robert was rather better served: his likeness was captured in two miniatures by Samuel Cooper, one now in the Fitzwilliam Museum in Cambridge, and the other in the Victoria and Albert in London. Fine as they are, it must be said that there is very little similarity between these portraits of Robert, and they could easily be taken for pictures of quite different men. Both show head and shoulders only, which is quite usual for a miniature, and in both pictures Robert is wearing armour, with a plain white linen collar softening the martial effect.

As Pauline Gregg remarked, Glover's engraving of John Lilburne looks more like the portrait of a Cavalier poet than that of a tough military man, jail-bird and political agitator. To judge by their portraits, both John and Robert had rather large skulls in proportion to their faces, something which can make any head seem a little immature. In the V&A miniature of Robert, the top of his head seems so high that one suspects that at one point he may have suffered from a mild case of hydrocephalus, or water on the brain.

John Lilburne's delicate good looks were compromised by an accidental injury to his eye, caused by the sharp end of a military pike, one of the standard battlefield weapons of the day. He lost his sight in that eye as a result of the accident, and was lucky not to have lost his life. From that point on, he wore glasses. Of course neither of the surviving engraved portraits can show us the scars that must have remained on his back after his flogging in 1638.

As we know, the 1649 engraved portrait of John Lilburne serves as the frontispiece to a book recounting the details of Lilburne's trial of the same year. The outcome of the trial was good for him both personally and for his wider cause. The frontispiece also shows both sides of a celebratory medal struck for the occasion.

Many of the books and pamphlets that were so poorly printed at the time were by their nature ephemeral: they were written and printed to report on, or in response to, a specific political event or situation. Sometimes they were written as a response to a previous pamphlet or pamphlets which the author or authors wanted to contradict, or support.

At times, any piece of writing that came to hand seemed to be considered worthy of publication, including personal letters, legal documents and long illustrative extracts from older writings. Pamphlets were often very poorly focused in terms of their content. In his 1649 *Legal Fundamental Liberties*, for instance, Lilburne prefaced a useful account of his life up to the point of writing with a lengthy attack on both Parliament and Oliver Cromwell.

Many of these flimsy tracts must have been thrown away, used as kindling or even pressed into service as hair-curlers after they had been read. A large number did, however, survive thanks to the efforts of George Thomason, a London bookseller who collected over twenty thousand books and tracts between 1640 and 1661. The so-called Thomason Tracts are now held by the British Library, but they have long been available on microfilm and online.

By turning from attacking the king and the bishops to attacking the House of Commons, which was then supported and dominated by Puritans, John Lilburne was turning some of his old Puritan friends into enemies. One of these was John Bastwick, whose seditious writings Lilburne had been accused of importing into England; and William Prynne, who had suffered even worse punishments for publishing forbidden books than Lilburne himself. The authorities believed that Prynne had attacked both kings and bishops in his writings, and as a result he had his ears brutally cropped, his nose slit, and the letters 'S' and 'L' branded on his cheeks. The letters were supposed to stand for 'Seditious Libeller'.

John Lilburne took exception to a tract Prynne had published in 1645. This was his *Truth Triumphing Over Falsehood, Antiquity*

Over Novelty, in which he had argued for:

the undoubted ecclesiastical jurisdiction, right, legislative, coercive power of Christian emperors, kings, magistrates, parliaments, in all matters of religion, church-government, discipline, ceremonies, manners . . .

Lilburne quickly answered this with his pamphlet *A Copy of a Letter . . . to Mr William Prynne* in which he set out his own ideas about how churches should be governed. Lilburne's stance on this subject were consistent with his adherence to the Independent strain of Protestant Christianity at the time, which held that individual churches should be able to discern for themselves how Christ wanted them to conduct themselves, and should certainly not be dominated by 'emperors, kings, magistrates' or 'parliaments'.

From the twenty-first century perspective, it may seem odd that so much ink should be spilt on arguments about how churches should be organised; but as M.A. Gibb points out in her 1947 biography of Lilburne, ideas about this apparently irrelevant matter tended to sit beside other political and philosophical ideas in the minds of thinkers like Prynne and Lilburne. In modern times, these historic concerns are still reflected in the names of different Christian denominations: Presbyterian, Congregational, Episcopalian, even 'wee free'.

Writers on Lilburne and his times often note how Puritan opinion in England seemed to divide during the Civil Wars. Independents like Lilburne found themselves in opposition to the Presyterians in Parliament and elsewhere who, partly because of Scottish influence, wanted local churches to have to answer to an overarching hierarchy, though not one dominated by the hated bishops. The implication in Prynne's *Truth Triumphing Over Falsehood* was that a national government, whether or not it was answerable to an emperor, king, magistrate or parliament, should be in overall charge of this church hierarchy. This Lilburne could not accept.

John Bastwick, who favoured a type of Presbyterianism that was opposed to Lilburne's views on church government, and

Colonel Edward King, whose faults as a soldier Lilburne had made known to Cromwell, saw a chance to attack John one summer day at Westminster. On the nineteenth of July 1645, King and Bastwick happened to spot Lilburne there, and informed the House of Commons that the northerner was spreading accusations against the then Speaker of the House, William Lenthall.

Lilburne was arrested, and despite the trumped-up nature of the charges, based on malicious gossip, he was kept in Newgate Prison until October the fourteenth. During his last days in prison, he published *England's Birthright Justified*, in which he complained about his unfair treatment, and the manner in which Parliament was investigating Speaker Lenthall, the man against whom Lilburne is supposed to have plotted:

. . . sometimes, while they are sitting about the examination of his treason . . . he shall sit down beside them with his hat on, as if he were one of them, and . . . he shall enjoy from the committee ten times more favour and respect, than the just, honest, and legal informers against him; who by some of the committees themselves, while they are sitting, are threatened, jeered, nick-named, and otherways most shamefully abused.

Also in *England's Birthright Justified*, Lilburne railed against the monopoly enjoyed by the Merchant Adventurers, which had made it impossible for him to take up his old master's profession of cloth-merchant when he left the army. Lilburne also objected to the monopoly on printing enjoyed by the Stationers, whom he characterised as 'malignant fellows' who were determined:

to suppress everything which hath any true declaration of the just rights and liberties of the free-born people of this nation, and to brand and traduce all such writers and writings with the odious terms of sedition, conspiracy and treason.

VI. Against the House of Lords

Not for the first time, Elizabeth Lilburne lived with her husband in prison during his months in Newgate. She no doubt reflected that if John had taken the government job she had secured for him in 1642, they would have been living in a fine house, like Lilburne's uncle George, rather than a jail. After his (or their) release in October 1645 it was not long before Lilburne was threatened with prison again.

In 1646 Edward King, the colonel whom Lilburne had found to be so incompetent and corrupt, was still waiting to be tried for high treason by the House of Lords when he brought a charge of slander against Lilburne in the Court of Common Pleas. As he had done when he was accused of smuggling illegal pamphlets in 1637, Lilburne defended himself by picking holes in the case brought against him, and by questioning the right of the court to try him at all. In a tract called *The Just Man's Justification*, he pointed out that it was surely wrong for Colonel King, who knew that Lilburne would be a witness against him in his treason trial, to be able to silence him by lodging an accusation against him with a lower court.

The Just Man's Justification began as a printed version of a letter from Lilburne to Justice Reeves, 'one of the justices of the commonwealth's courts, commonly called Common Pleas'; but as happened in many of Lilburne's tracts, it wandered off the point and became an outspoken text which was bound to offend the House of Lords. As well as repeating Lilburne's old accusations against Colonel King, and asserting that his slander charge was

34

nothing more than a ruse, *The Just Man's Justification* criticised the earl of Manchester, who had been both Lilburne and King's commanding officer, and was now the Speaker of the House of Lords. Taking a wider historical view, Lilburne also suggested that both houses of parliament, and many other institutions, as well as most of the laws of England, were alien and tyrannical innovations introduced by William the Conqueror and his successors. 'The main stream of our common law,' Lilburne writes, 'with the practice thereof, flowed out of Normandy, notwithstanding all objections can be made to the contrary, and therefore I say it came from the will of a tyrant'.

The House of Lords knew about the publication of Lilburne's *Just Man's Justification* in advance of his appearance before them on the eleventh of June 1646. Manchester, his old commander, had a copy of it shown to John and asked him if he was familiar with it. In reply, Lilburne asked to see a written copy of the charge against him. When their Lordships insisted that he answer their question, the prisoner produced the 'protestation' he had written during a pause on his way to the House that morning. The Lords would not accept the paper, and Lilburne would not take it when they tried to give it back to him. As he left, they threw the paper after him.

'Being not long without,' Lilburne tells us in his tract *The Freeman's Freedom Vindicated*, 'the Gentleman usher came civilly to me, and told me I must put off my sword and give it to some of my friends, for I must go a prisoner to Newgate'.

Lilburne's protestation, which the Lords had tried so hard to ignore, was soon printed as part of *The Freeman's Freedom Vindicated*. It asserted that, since he was a commoner, under the provisions of Magna Carta the Lords had no right to try him. Lilburne added that:

I do hereby declare and am resolved as in duty bound to God, my self, country, and posterity, to maintain my legal liberties, to the last drop of my blood, against all opposers whatsoever

This was fighting talk, and the Lords would have got another hint about Lilburne's warlike intentions in an earlier part of *The*

Freeman's Freedom, where he reported part of a conversation he had with a member of their Lordships' house before he appeared before them. Lilburne told this unnamed man that:

> if he and the rest of the Lords endeavoured to destroy Magna Carta and to tread it under their feet, as they would do if they meddled with me in this case, I would draw my sword against them every man as freely as I would do against the king, and the desperatest Cavalier with him

Elsewhere in *The Freeman's Freedom Vindicated*, Lilburne attacked his:

> . . . old back friend the Earl of Manchester, the fountain (as I conceive) of all my present troubles, who would have hanged me for taking a castle from the Cavaliers in Yorkshire; but is so closely glued in interest to that party, that he protected from justice Colonel King, one of his own officers, for his good service in treacherously delivering or betraying Crowland to the Cavaliers, and never called, nor that I could hear, desired to call to account his officer, or officers, that basely, cowardly, and treacherously, betrayed and delivered Lincoln last up to the enemy, without striking one stroke, or staying till so much as a troop of horse, or a trumpeter came to demand it, his lordship's head hath stood it seems too long upon his shoulders . . .

Despite its convoluted grammar, this was a clear attack on both Colonel King and the earl of Manchester, who, the author implies, should be beheaded as soon as possible. Since, as we know, Manchester was then Speaker of the Lords, and since Lilburne was characterising the Lords' treatment of him as a gross affront to 'legal liberties', it is hardly surprising that their Lordships should have felt it necessary to send John back to Newgate. Lilburne confirmed his status as a threat to the House of Lords during his next appearance there, when he threatened to burn the place down. After another appearance before their Lordships, Lilburne was transferred to the Tower of London, after he had stopped his ears so that he could not hear their speeches to him, and refused to kneel to them.

In theory, Lilburne's confinement in the Tower was supposed to be very strict, with no pen, ink or paper, and no visitors, not even his wife. A bribe of fifteen shillings a week, paid to his gaoler, relaxed things, however, and there was soon a steady stream of writings coming from the prisoner.

His new imprisonment renewed John Lilburne's status as a *cause célèbre*. Among those who rallied to his cause was William Walwyn, who may have encountered Lilburne for the first time on the very day in 1645 when he was arrested at Westminster and imprisoned because of his opposition to William Lenthall, Speaker of the House of Commons. Back then, Walwyn had come to his new friend's defence with a tract called *England's Lamentable Slavery*. In 1647, Walwyn also published *A Pearl in a Dunghill* in an attempt to show up the injustice of Lilburne's new imprisonment. The author published his *Pearl* so quickly that it was in circulation before John was transferred from Newgate to the Tower.

Walwyn, who was some ten or fifteen years older than Lilburne, came from a similar background to John's, though their personalities could hardly have been more different. Like Lilburne the second son of a landed gentlemen, Walwyn was also apprenticed to a Londoner engaged in the rag trade – in William's case a silk merchant in Paternoster Row. Like Lilburne, Walwyn also married a merchant's daughter, but unlike John, William was able to make a dependable living from a trade – in his case that of a weaver.

A wide reader like Lilburne, Walwyn became interested in religious questions and began to publish tracts with titles like *Good Counsel to All*, *The Compassionate Samaritan* (both 1644), *A Parable* and *Toleration Justified* (both 1646). In this time of sectarian strife, the weaver wrote in defence of religious toleration, even toleration of a person 'whose mind', as he wrote in *Toleration Justified*, 'is so misinformed as to deny a deity'.

Although Walwyn's tolerant view of different religious viewpoints seems to have originated from his amiable disposition and relaxed broad-mindedness, he was very much ahead of his time in many respects, and seen by some as a dangerous extremist.

He supported the Roundhead side in the Civil War because he believed that a Parliamentary victory would secure the rights and liberties that would allow himself and his fellow citizens to live in a more enlightened state, different from the state he saw in 1646, where

there brake forth here about London a spirit of persecution; whereby private meetings were molested, and divers pastors of congregations imprisoned, and all threatened

(from *Walwyn's Just Defence*, 1649)

Walwyn's *Pearl in a Dunghill*, written in 1647 to protest against Lilburne's new imprisonment, insisted, as Lilburne himself had done, that the Lords had no right to try a commoner like Lilburne. The tract also reminded its readers of the sufferings Lilburne had already undergone at the hands of the bishops, who had caused him to be:

imprisoned in the Fleet by a most cruel and barbarous sentence, which they procured in the Star Chamber against him, and so was whipped, gagged and pilloried, yea and in his close imprisonment almost famished and murdered

A Pearl in a Dunghill also alludes to Lilburne's war-service, when:

. . . under the Earl of Manchester . . . with the loss both of his blood, estate and many hazards of his life, he . . . performed noble services, as the taking of Tickhill Castle, Sir John Wortley's house and the like, in all which, malice itself cannot accuse him either of cowardice or covetousness.

Walwyn suggests that, by contrast, the Lords were of little use during the war, and that Cromwell's New Model Army was a force to be reckoned with because there was 'not one lord' in it. The author insists that the House of Commons must step in, 'instantly deliver this just man' and 'reduce the Lords to a condition suitable to the freedom of the people, and consistent with the freedom of parliaments'.

VII. Allies

Walwyn's *A Pearl in a Dunghill* depicts Lilburne's unjust imprisonment by the Lords as a symptom of the disappointing state of affairs in England, after the king had been captured by the Parliamentary side, and Parliament reigned supreme. Later pamphlets by Walwyn, Lilburne and others would continue the theme of bitter disappointment and disillusionment: how could injustice and oppression still be thriving when the king was out of the picture, and the House of Commons, elected by the people, was 'The Supreme Power'?

In *A Pearl*, Walwyn hints at a possible reason for the continued underhand dealing of both houses of parliament:

Is it not because there is a Popish and Episcopal party under other pretences as busy working in the kingdom now as ever? And as he [Lilburne] was a special instrument of the bishops' overthrow, so those their agents are the prime causers and workers both of his ruin, and all that will take his part, if possibly they could once get that decree scaled and un-altered, so that there should not be separate or sectary any more mentioned.

A similar conspiracy theory is set out in a tract written by one Richard Overton, with help from William Walwyn, also published to protest against Lilburne's new imprisonment. In *A Remonstrance of Many Thousand Citizens*, Overton suggests that a breed of malcontents, dissatisfied with their lowly positions under King Charles I, took advantage of the increased 'oppressions' of the king to turn everything upside-down and put themselves in power. Now, Overton suggests, the malcontents are holding out against real reform until 'the people by degrees are tired and wearied, so as they shall not be able to contest or dispute with us either about supreme or inferior power'. This strategy, Overton suggests, is one of the 'hidden things' that 'time has revealed'.

Throughout his *Remonstrance*, Overton makes frequent mention of 'the mystery of iniquity', an idea from the New Testament second letter to the Thessalonians (2 Thess. 2:7). In this passage, the author of the letter prophesies that, before Christ can return again, there must be 'a falling away', when 'the son of perdition' will gain power, and there will be much delusion.

Beyond the rather diffuse suggestions that the Commons must support liberty, work for the release of Lilburne and limit the power of the Lords, Walwyn's *Pearl* does not offer much in the way of suggestions for reform, though it paints a lively picture of how bad things had got under parliamentary rule. The pamphlet does, however, end with a vague threat that the English 'are become a knowing and judicious people', made wise by affliction, who would 'abominate' any attempt to make slaves of them, as they would abominate murder and betrayal.

Overton's threats in his *Remonstrance* are rather more specific and alarming. God himself, Overton asserts, will punish those who perpetuate injustice, 'for God will not be mocked nor suffer such gross hypocrisy to pass without exemplary punishment'. The people, Overton adds, will be paying more attention to both houses of parliament in future, and parliamentarians can expect to hear more from the people who elected them. Writing as if he were himself a sort of god formed out of the will of the people, Overton demands parliaments elected annually, more transparency and fair dealing in government, and thoroughgoing reforms of many aspects of political life. Only thus, he implies, can the gross injustice of the alien ways of the Norman invaders be purged out of the system, when 'we shall not doubt to be made absolute freemen in time, and become a just, plenteous and powerful nation'.

To Overton, Magna Carta, to which John Lilburne was so devoted, was 'a beggarly thing containing many marks of intolerable bondage'. He asserts that:

the laws of this nation are unworthy a free people and deserve from first to last to be considered and seriously debated, and reduced to an agreement with common equity and right reason, which ought to be the form and life of every government

It is clear that Overton and many who shared his opinions wanted this 'agreement' to be something like a constitution or bill of rights, upon which a new and better system of government and law would be built. The celebrated first *Agreement of the People*, partly authored by Richard Overton himself, appeared in the winter of the year after Lilburne was sent to the Tower.

Despite years of scholarly probing, Richard Overton remains one of the more mysterious members of Lilburne's group. He may have been some fifteen years older than Lilburne himself, and the interest in rural affairs that is shown in many of his writings may suggest a country upbringing, perhaps in Lincolnshire.

It is possible that Overton was rather better-educated than Lilburne, and had studied at Queen's College Cambridge. He may have been a Church of England curate at one time, but later became a Baptist. In an age where prose-writers were forever tripping over their long sentences, Overton's *Remonstrance* showcases the author's ability to fire off short, sharply-pointed phrases that force the reader to sit up. Examples include, 'we are your principals, and you our agents', 'but it would not do', 'longer they would not bear' and 'let the righteous God judge between you and us'.

The sense of bitter disappointment, expressed at this time in pamphlets by Walwyn, Overton, Lilburne and others, was particularly marked among the soldiers of the Parliamentarian army. Like Lilburne himself, many of these men had abandoned homes, families, gainful employment and, in some cases, worthwhile businesses to fight the king. Now, with the war over, they found that they were enjoying little or no share of the spoils; royal tyranny was being replaced with parliamentary tyranny, Lilburne himself was a captive again, the Long Parliament was still in power, there was still a House of Lords, and there was even a chance that the king would be restored to his throne. The fact that something like Scottish-style Presbyterianism was now dominating English politics was also disturbing to numbers in the army, many of whom were Independents like Lilburne himself, and hankered after a much more democratic system of government than seemed to be on the table.

On the bread-and-cheese level, many of the Roundhead troopers were owed a great deal of back-pay, and it seemed that Parliament was intent on disbanding them before any of this was distributed. The army also wanted to be indemnified against future prosecution for crimes committed during the war. Men who had been ordered to ransack a Royalist's house for supplies, for example, did not want to be prosecuted for theft by the Royalist owner of the house.

In August 1647 the army seized the City of London, intent on pressurising the government into accepting the reforms proposed in the aforementioned *Agreement of the People*; a text that was heavily influenced by the ideas of Lilburne and his followers.

The purpose of the first, November 1647, *Agreement of the People* was clearly stated in its sub-title: 'for a firm and present peace, upon grounds of common rights'. Having fought for freedom 'by our late labours and hazards' the army felt it part of their duty to promote a new system of government that would frustrate the efforts of those 'that seek to make themselves our masters' and plotted to restore 'our former oppressions'.

The 1647 *Agreement* proposed what we would now call constituency boundary changes, to make Parliament fairer and more representative. Elections to this parliament were to be held every two years, beginning after the Long Parliament was dissolved on the date the *Agreement* proposed, at the end of September 1648. According to the *Agreement*, this September day would see an end to inquiries into and lawsuits arising from 'anything said or done, in reference to the late public differences', meaning war-crimes. This new form of parliament would have a great deal of power in certain areas, such as law-making and waging war; power that could not be interfered with by mighty interests outside of Parliament itself. Likewise, laws passed by Parliament would apply to everyone, regardless of 'tenure, estate, charter, degree, birth, or place'. The new House of Commons would not, however, be able to legislate to force people to abandon their own version of Christianity, or use conscription to recruit a new army.

The proposals contained in the first *Agreement of the People* were discussed in the famous Putney Debates during late October and early November 1647. At these discussions, the 'army grandees', as they were known, were represented by the leading general, Henry Ireton, and his father-in-law, Oliver Cromwell. Ireton in particular found that he could not agree to the wider suffrage that the supporters of the *Agreement* favoured. At that time, only adult male owners of property worth over forty shillings a year could vote in parliamentary elections in England. Ireton felt that the inclusion of less wealthy voters would endanger the property of people like himself. Both Ireton and Cromwell were also cautious about the other reforms proposed in the *Agreement*, which would have made Parliament all-powerful, and limited the role of senior army officers, the Lords and, crucially, the king.

At that time, Cromwell and others were still negotiating with King Charles, who was imprisoned at Hampton Court. True to form, Charles was also negotiating with Royalist elements in England and Scotland, although some would characterise these 'negotiations' as 'plotting' pure and simple. Fearing, perhaps, that developments such as the *Agreement of the People* and the subsequent Putney Debates might lead to the loss of both his role and his head, the king made an unsuccessful attempt to escape, on the eleventh of November 1647. Although Charles was quickly recaptured, his escape was followed by a Scottish invasion, and Royalist uprisings in England, and the soldiers abandoned their attempts at constitution-making, for the time being.

VIII. The Levellers

By the time of the first *Agreement of the People* and the subsequent Putney Debates, people were referring to the members of Lilburne's group as 'Levellers'. Lilburne himself always resisted the label, preferring to call himself an 'agitator'; and although the term continues to be used by historians, it is a misleading misnomer.

Surely 'Leveller' implies someone who wants to 'level out' the wealth and power of a whole population, so that everyone ends up the same. This was how the contemporary Royalist chronicler Edward Hyde, Earl of Clarendon understood the term 'Leveller' as applied to Lilburne and his group. In his monumental *History of the Rebellion* Clarendon stated that the Levellers declared 'that all degrees of men should be levelled, and an equality should be established, both in titles and estates throughout the kingdoms'.

Although, at the Putney Debates, Henry Ireton aired his concerns that the Leveller-inspired *Agreement of the People*, if enshrined in law, might have that effect, this kind of 'levelling' was never an aspiration for John Lilburne. He would surely have been very angry if some seventeenth-century commissar had marched onto the family lands in County Durham and seized them for the people. Although the Levellers so-called certainly were concerned about poverty and inequality, their main concern was to remove the corrupt legal practices that put men like Lilburne himself in prison for no good reason. To counter such abuses, they knew that they needed to introduce reforms that would make the law, and government itself, transparent, responsive, relevant and above all fair.

The one seventeenth-century group that really deserved to wear the 'Leveller' label was the so-called Diggers, who quite rightly called themselves 'True Levellers'. Their leader was a visionary Lancashire man called Gerrard Winstanley. Born at Wigan, Winstanley, like Lilburne, was apprenticed, as a youth, to a London merchant. Like John, Gerrard was able to read widely as a London apprentice, though his contact with radical elements in London during his apprenticeship, and after he had set up his own modest business in the capital, seems to have been insignificant. Like Lilburne, Winstanley failed as a businessman, but instead of escaping into the army and political agitation, the man from Wigan took himself and his wife off to live near her father at Cobham in Surrey.

Gerrard was no more successful in his country business than in his city one, and during 1647 and '48 he suffered a financial collapse, and a spiritual re-birth. He took to writing religious books which attempted to put the alarming political and military situation of the time into a Christian context. Like Richard Overton, Winstanley wrote about the 'mystery of iniquity', and discerned signs of the Apocalypse and the Second Coming in the political divisions of the time.

Winstanley believed that enlightened people should prepare for the imminent new age of righteousness by dispensing with superfluous material wealth and social hierarchies. Just a few weeks after King Charles I was beheaded, Winstanley and a small group of followers started to dig up a piece of common land at St George's Hill near Cobham, planning to sow parsnips, carrots and beans. Soon, other Digger communities were appearing in Buckinghamshire, Northamptonshire and Essex.

Local pressure to get the Diggers off St George's Hill began almost immediately, and soon Winstanley's group was forced to relocate to Little Heath in Cobham itself. In April 1650 John Platt, the local parson, led some fifty men in an attack on the Digger settlement, burning down six houses or shelters. By the next autumn, the Cobham Diggers were looking for work threshing other people's wheat.

Winstanley's Digger experiment had failed, but instead of choosing the life of an embittered rebel, he became a respected, fairly conventional figure in both Cobham and London. Although he had railed against the corrupting effects of money and the ownership of land in a series of tracts, the one-time Digger-in-chief now gained control of property at Cobham, and traded in corn in London. He also became a useful part of the local government down in Surrey, being put in charge of the care of the poor, and later becoming a church warden; though by the time of his death in 1676 he had become a Quaker.

Although, like Winstanley, John Lilburne became a Quaker in later life, it seems that Lilburne's personality would not allow him to settle down as Winstanley did, once it became evident that his great cause was lost. Gerrard had taken the execution of King Charles I in January 1649 as a sign that a new, free and radical form of government would soon turn England into a sort of egalitarian paradise. Almost exactly a year after his followers had started to dig up St George's Hill, Winstanley was forced to face the fact that the titles, names and faces at the top had changed, but that the people at or near the bottom were still as powerless and down-trodden as ever.

John Lilburne may have done well to take the events from 1648 to 1650 as his cue to stop barking up his accustomed tree. In December 1648 Colonel Thomas Pride had marched into Parliament and conducted 'Pride's Purge', excluding any members who were not sympathetic to the army, and thereby creating the so-called 'Rump' Parliament. The Rump went on to vote to try King Charles. Soon the House of Lords and the monarchy itself were abolished. This meant that, having previously been tried by the Star Chamber, John Lilburne had been tried by two bodies that were later abolished.

The new arrangements for the government of the country, which also featured a Council of State that was dominated by the army, concentrated a great deal of power in the hands of the army grandees. Some historians regard the Council of State of the time as nothing more than a military junta. In climbing up to power over the dead body of Charles I, Cromwell and the other army leaders had put aside ideas such as those contained in the Leveller-inspired 1647 *Agreement of the People*. This provoked a new torrent of critical pamphlets from Lilburne and his followers.

John had been released from the Tower in August 1648, but he was back there again, with Overton, Walwyn and another Leveller called Thomas Prince, less than eight months later. The foursome were accused of having published a pamphlet called *The Second Part of England's New Chains*, which appeared in March 1649. No authors' names appeared on the tract – they were only identified as 'several well-affected persons inhabiting the city of London, Westminster, the borough of Southwark, Hamlets, and places adjacent'. Addressing themselves to 'the representors of the people, in parliament assembled', the authors lamented the 'present miseries and approaching dangers of the nation' and also 'the misery, danger, and bondage threatened'. According to the 'well-affected persons' the new all-powerful parliament was re-imposing 'oppressions' of the type previously identified with 'the king and bishops'. The men now in power, it was implied, were like physicians who had been tasked with healing the state, but who had only made it sicker. The new oppressors resembled the old ones in many things, including their use of slanderous labels such as 'Leveller'.

Looking back, the pamphlet notes how 'powerful and ever-ruling influences' had frustrated the best hopes of the army and the people: these 'influences' only worked to satisfy their own 'lusts, pride and domination'. Turning to specifics, the authors relate how Henry Lilburne, John's younger brother, described here as a 'perfidious traitor', was persuaded to convince King Charles that there was a plot afoot to assassinate him – a plot led by John Lilburne himself. This information supposedly persuaded the king to escape from Hampton Court, only to be re-captured and imprisoned on the Isle of Wight. This was done, according to *The Second Part of England's New Chains*, so that the 'powerful and ever-ruling influences' could 'entirely possess' the king.

Among further accusations, the 1649 tract hints at a deadly plot hatched by the 'influences' against Thomas Rainborowe (often written 'Rainsborough'). Rainborowe was a remarkably successful

Roundhead army colonel, who was also a Leveller, and had spoken with great power and eloquence in favour of the *Agreement of the People* at the Putney debates. The official story of his death stated that while he was at Doncaster during the Second Civil War in October 1648, a group of Cavaliers burst in on him, intending to take him prisoner. But Rainborowe fought back and was killed in the struggle. In *The Second Part of England's New Chains,* the authors hint that everything about the official account of these events was suspicious, and that the authors' suspicions are heightened by the fact that an attempt by Rainborowe's brother to investigate the matter 'receives no furtherance, but rather, all discouragement that may be'. Rainborowe was certainly no friend of Oliver Cromwell's, and the elimination of such a well-regarded army Leveller would have been greeted as good news among the 'powerful and ever-ruling influences'.

Shortly after Lilburne, Overton, Walwyn and Prince had been arrested for the publication of *The Second Part of England's New Chains* in March 1649, they were questioned by the new Council of State, then put into an ante-chamber to wait while the Council debated their case. By pressing his ear to the door, Lilburne was able to hear Cromwell 'thumping his fist upon the council table', and bellowing that 'you have no other way to deal with these men, but to break them in pieces'. He went on, 'if you do not break them, they will break you'.

The regime attempted to 'break' Lilburne with a new treason trial, conducted at the Guildhall in London in October 1649. As at his trial before the Star Chamber in 1638, Lilburne refused to cooperate with the court, though this time he was better-read and more experienced, and the outcome was much better for him. He questioned the court's right to try him, and criticised the very existence of the court, as well as the manner in which the judges had been appointed to it.

He demanded a legal advisor, and complained that he could not read the indictment that had been sent to him because it was written in Latin and in a very unusual script (the next year, 1650, a law was passed stipulating that all legal documents must be in English). He demanded that the indictment should be read out in court, which later happened. He also claimed that he had been arrested in the wrong way by the wrong set of officers; and poured scorn on the recently-framed law under which he had been charged.

At times during the three days of the trial, John Lilburne seemed to be completely in control of proceedings, objecting to witnesses and questions, and even asking the spectators crowded into the Guildhall to keep quiet. Most of those watching the trial seem to have been on his side, and when the jury found him not guilty 'the people unanimously shouted for half an hour without intermission'. Bonfires were lit in celebration, and the aforementioned medal was struck, both sides of which are shown in the engraved frontispiece to the printed account of the trial.

D: Baſtwick, for writing a Booke againſt Po;
piſh-Biſhops was firſt fined 1000ⁱ and Commit;
ted Cloſe-priſoner in the Gatehouſe, by the high
Commiſsion. After that for writing of the Pari;
ty of Miniſters, &c, was cenſured in the Starr;
Chamber to be depriued of his practiſe in Phy;
ſick. to looſe both his Eares in the pillorie, was
fined 5000ⁱ baniſhed into the Iſle of Sillyes
and there Committed to perpetuall cloſe im;
priſonment, where hee was moſt cruelly u;
ſed, and no freinds, no not ſo much as his
wife or Children once permitted to ſee him
on pain of impriſonment, as afore ſaid.

W. Hollar fecit

John Bastwick, by Wenceslaus Hollar (Wellcome Collection)

The Tower of London, also by Hollar

The Star Chamber in 1873

Archbishop William Laud

Charles I after an engraving by Van Dyck (Wellcome)

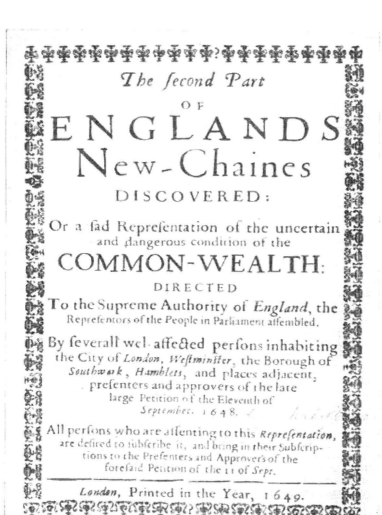

The second Part

OF

ENGLANDS

New-Chaines

DISCOVERED:

Or a fad Reprefentation of the uncertain
and dangerous condition of the

COMMON-WEALTH:

DIRECTED

To the Supreme Authority of *England*, the
Reprefentors of the People in Parliament affembled.

By feverall wel-affe&ed perfons inhabiting
the City of *London*, *Weftminfter*, the Borough of
Southwark, *Hamblets*, and places adjacent,
prefenters and approvers of the late
large Petition of the Eleventh of
September. 1648.

All perfons who are affenting to this *Reprefentation*,
are defired to fubfcribe it, and bring in their Subfcrip-
tions to the Prefenters and Approvers of the
forefaid Petition of the 11 of *Sept.*

London, Printed in the Year, 1649.

Title page of the Second Part of England's New Chains, 1649

Oliver Cromwell (Wellcome)

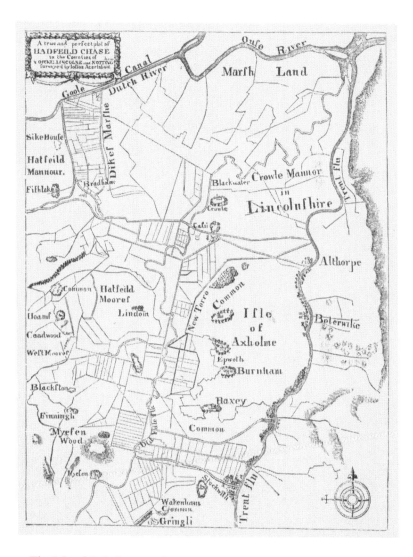

The Isle of Axholme etc. from Samuel Smiles' Lives of the Engineers

Lilburne on trial (British Library)

George Villiers

Charles II (Wellcome)

IX. Lawyer for Hire

Free again, again John Lilburne had to find a new way to make money. Having failed as a brewer, and been excluded from the profession of clothier, he turned to making soap; called soap-boiling at the time. Of course he quickly found himself getting involved in a protest against an unfair tax on soap.

As a celebrated London resident with a reputation for speaking truth to power, Lilburne was elected by a clear majority to the post of Common Councillor of the City of London. To be admitted to this prestigious position, Lilburne had to 'take the Engagement', meaning that he had to undertake to be faithful to the new government. Those who took the Engagement promised to 'be true and faithful to the Commonwealth of England, as it is now established, without a King or House of Lords'. Lilburne took it, but asserted that he had not meant to swear to be faithful to 'the present Parliament, Council of State, or Council of the Army'. As a result of this assertion, his election was quashed.

Whether or not soap-boiling paid well, Lilburne also became an amateur lawyer at this time. He was not permitted to enter the profession formally, but his reputation as a man with knowledge and experience of the law brought him some important clients. He became involved in the case of one John Poytz, who in 1648 had been imprisoned and heavily fined by the House of Lords for forging an Act of Parliament. In 1650, after the abolition of the Lords, and with the help of Lilburne and his friend John Wildman, Poyntz petitioned 'the supreme authority, the Parliament of the

Commonwealth'. Poyntz's petition gives the impression that in this case at least Lilburne was acting as a poor man's lawyer. The petitioner claims that he is 'now very poor' and that his rich enemies 'are able to give many and great fees'. The 'professed lawyers' are 'unwilling to take any pains' in his case, and so Poyntz begs that 'some honest gentlemen . . . may have favourable audience'. Poyntz also claimed that the cheap professional lawyers he had engaged were easily over-awed by the kind his better-off enemies could hire.

Poyntz had used his (probably forged) Act of Parliament in a property dispute in Essex. Also in 1650, Lilburne, again with John Wildman, became involved in a complex land dispute centred on the Isle of Axholme in Lincolnshire. The case was similar in some respects to the 1649 dispute at St George's Hill in Surrey between the locals and Gerrard Winstanley's Diggers. In the Lincolnshire case, the locals, who claimed an ancient right to use common land, were protesting not against idealistic 'True Levellers' but against the government, and the share-holders in a fen drainage scheme.

The area had been drained by the Dutch engineer Cornelius Vermuyden between 1626 and 1629, during the early years of the reign of Charles I. From the king's point of view, the main reason for the draining of the area was to dry out Hatfield Chase, a royal hunting-ground where, before Vermuyden got to work, princely Nimrods had been obliged to hunt deer from boats. Vanmuyden had first been brought to England in 1621 to repair a breach in the Thames embankment at Dagenham. In his book *Lives of the Engineers*, Samuel Smiles explains why the English frequently called on the Dutch for such work:

No people had fought against water so boldly, so perseveringly, and so successfully. They had made their own land out of the mud of the rest of Europe, and, being rich and prosperous, were ready to enter upon similar enterprises in other countries.

As Charles Wilson says in his book *Holland and Britain*, 'the Dutch technician was to the seventeenth century what the Scotch engineer was to the nineteenth'.

Before Vermuyden's advent, Axholme had been a true inland island, surrounded by water; rather similar, in fact, to Cornelius's homeland of Tholen in Zealand. Some parts of Axholme were only ever accessible by boat: the wetlands these vessels navigated were rich in fish and waterfowl, and were a great resource for the locals, the so-called 'Isleonians'.

At the start of the seventeenth century, some areas around Axholme were only flooded in the winter: in the summer they became common pasture-land and a valuable source of peat, used as fuel. The locals claimed that their legal right to the use of these common lands went back to 1359.

King Charles had never intended to pay Vermuyden directly for his work: instead he granted him a third of the newly-drained land. In turn, the Dutchman sold much of this land to share-holders, who became known as the Participants. Many of these newcomers were themselves Dutch, and many locals believed that more of the land they were now claiming as theirs should have remained as common land. Unfortunately, there was a nasty tinge of xenophobia in some of the locals' attitude to the incomers. The Isleonians had not been happy about the mistakes Vermuyden had made in the early days of the project, and they remained unhappy about the re-allocation of land, and the amount of compensation some of them had been paid.

Many Isleonians associated the drainage scheme, that had left so many of them out of pocket, with King Charles, so that when the First Civil War began in 1642 they took the law into their own hands and began to use Participants' land as if it were still common land. This resembled the way that the Diggers had taken the execution of the king as a cue to invade St George's Hill in Surrey. The Lincolnshire agitators tried to return their landscape to its natural state by demolishing banks built to hold back water, and filling up drainage ditches with earth. They then let their cattle loose to graze on the private crops and pastures of the Participants.

Later, the Lincolnshire protesters destroyed flood-gates, embankments and sluices, damaging some four thousand acres. In response, the Participants petitioned Parliament, demanding help. The protesters might have hoped that, since they had supported

Parliament during the Civil Wars, and the Participants had sided with the king, Parliament might sympathise with their side. This was not what happened: the Sheriff of Lincoln was sent in with a force of a hundred men.

By this time a solicitor called Daniel Noddell was leading the agitators, and he had *four* hundred men at his back. Noddell's followers undid the repairs the sheriff's men had made, and laid waste another three thousand four hundred acres in the Epworth area.

By this time, Noddell had gained the assistance of John Lilburne and his friend John Wildman. When Parliament decreed, in 1650, that the Participants were in the right, the Isleonians declared that they were 'a parliament of clouts' and proceeded to demolish the village of Sandtoft, home to over eighty people, in the course of ten days. Laying waste houses, barns, stables and a windmill at Sandtoft, the agitators also turned their attention to the local fields and wrecked rape and corn crops. They also vandalised the village church: first they took the valuable lead off the roof, removed all the seats, and buried carrion under the altar. Altogether, the damage at Sandtoft alone added up to some eighty thousand pounds, or over eight million today. Eventually John Lilburne himself lodged his servants in the village's partially-restored vicarage, and used the church as a stable and barn.

Noddell may have called on Lilburne and Wildman's help not because he needed legal advice but because he was looking for men prepared to share his leadership of what Shakespeare might have called 'a list of lawless resolutes'. Noddell might have thought that as army veterans, both of his new comrades would prove useful in a fight; and he knew that Lilburne in particular might write and publish a favourable account of the Isleonians' case. In fact Lilburne did exactly that, in 1651. That Lilburne had repeatedly proved himself fearless and outspoken in the face of authority might also have ticked an important box for Noddell.

It is hard to say exactly what Lilburne thought he would get out of his involvement with Noddell's local rebellion, beyond his fees as a lawyer. Lincolnshire was not his home, the dispute had already been going on for over twenty years, and Lilburne might have done well to remember the old saying about fools rushing in where angels fear to tread. Even with Lilburne and Wildman's assistance, Noddell's uprising did not succeed.

Another lawyer who had worked, like Noddell, for the Isleonians was Nathaniel Reading. He turned his coat and went to work for the Participants for a salary of two hundred pounds a year (over twenty thousand today). Reading contributed to the suppression of the agitators by calling in Edward Whalley, who had been a leading Roundhead officer during the Civil Wars. Since 1655, Whalley had been one of the ten major-generals appointed by Cromwell to rule the country during the so-called Protectorate. Whalley's bailiwick included Lincolnshire, and he applied military force to the problem of the unquiet commoners of Axholme Island.

With the help of the local sheriffs, Nathaniel Reading assembled a band of twenty armed men; mercenaries who were paid twenty pounds a year, and whose numbers could be increased at need. After thirty-one set battles against the rebellious locals, Reading was able to pacify the area, and repair the church at Sandtoft.

The Rev. W.R. Stonehouse, author of the 1839 *History and Topography of the Isle of Axholme* admired both Vermuyden and Nathaniel Reading, and even compared the latter to Hercules, the mythological hero. John Lilburne, however, he regarded as 'a person of most turbulent disposition', a 'stern republican' and 'one of the most restless and contentious spirits of the time'.

Stonehouse got his idea of both Lilburne and Wildman from the aforementioned *History of the Rebellion* by Clarendon. This meant that Stonehouse repeated a mistake of Clarendon's, who believed that 'obstinate and malicious' Lilburne was 'a poor bookbinder' at the start of the First Civil War. We see a milder Lilburne in the summer of 1650, expressing his thanks to Oliver Cromwell for his help in finally securing for him some of the money he was owed by Parliament. His gratitude, he wrote:

. . . flows not from a complimental but a real grateful acknowledgement of your Excellency's most obliging and noble favours manifested unto myself (after so many high and unfortunate misunderstandings betwixt us) in your late signal and most remarkable friendly carriage towards me, and in behalf, openly, and avowedly in the Council of State the day before you left London.

Also in this letter, Lilburne assured Cromwell that he had not been plotting with Royalists, and asserted that 'no man in England shall be more forward and ready to hazard his life with you and for you, in the face of ready to be discharged cannons and muskets, and all the dangers of the world'.

The letter refers to Cromwell's leaving London – this was the beginning of his ride north to fight the Scots, who had formed an uneasy alliance with the dead king's heir, who now regarded himself as King Charles II. On this occasion Lilburne did not 'hazard his life' for Cromwell 'in the face of ready to be discharged cannons and muskets', but he did ride north with him for twenty-five miles, and their leave-taking was most affectionate.

A turning-point in Cromwell's Scottish campaign of 1650 was the Battle of Dunbar, where the English prevailed partly because at a crucial point the muskets of the Scots were not 'ready to be discharged'. The matchlock guns of the time went off when a smouldering match was brought into contact with gunpowder, used as a propellant. One of the mistakes of the Scottish commanders at Dunbar was to instruct their men to put out their matches. When they also moved their force down from their commanding position Cromwell declared 'the Lord hath delivered them into our hands'.

X. Return to the North

One of the quirks of John Lilburne's character was surely his ability to fall in and out of friendship with other men. Many people would hesitate to fall out with some of the individuals Lilburne made into enemies, not just because such a falling-out could lead to bad feeling, but also because these were very powerful and dangerous individuals. By attacking erstwhile friends in his public statements, Lilburn not only gave offence, but also put himself and his family in danger. He could do this not just because of his fearlessness, but also because he seemed to care very little if he offended anyone, especially anyone in power.

It seems there was never much love lost between John Lilburne (or indeed any of the Durham Lilburnes) and Arthur Haselrig, a Leicestershire nobleman, Puritan, republican, Roundhead cavalry officer, and member of the Long Parliament and the Council of State. The Lilburnes had personal objections to Haselrig because when he became Governor of Newcastle in 1647 he replaced John Lilburne's brother Robert in the post. Also, as we know, in 1648 Haselrig re-took Tynemouth Castle, killing John's Royalist younger brother Henry Lilburne in the process. In 1650 Haselrig, who was responsible for paying back-rent to John Lilburne on lands the latter controlled in County Durham, refused to do so until John, in effect, challenged him to a duel.

Beyond putting Lilburne noses out of joint, there was much else for any enlightened person to object to in Haselrig's approach to his role as Governor of Newcastle; a role which also gave him a great deal of power south of the Tyne. After the Battle of Dunbar in

1650, the victorious Cromwell was left with perhaps five thousand Scottish prisoners on his hands. These were forced to participate in what can only be described as a death-march ninety miles south to the City of Durham.

At Newcastle, the prisoners became Arthur Haselrig's responsibility, and by various means their numbers had reduced to three thousand by the time they were imprisoned in Durham Cathedral. It is likely that as many as sixteen hundred died at Durham. Haselrig claimed, in a letter to the Council of State for Scottish and Irish affairs, that he had expended a great deal of money and effort on the care of these Scottish prisoners; but given the grim, grasping character of the man it seems likely that many of these deaths were due to his own callous negligence. When the graves of some of these men were discovered in 2015, examination of the bones revealed that their bodies had been denied Christian burial, and had even been dumped for a time in a place where rats could get to them.

According to the leading Parliamentarian Edmund Ludlow, Haselrig was 'a man of disobliging carriage, sour and morose of temper, liable to be transported with passion, and to whom liberality seemed to be a vice'. In 1650 one John Musgrave published a pamphlet about 'the great and heavy pressures and grievances' suffered by northerners under Haselrig's 'misgovernment', and in 1660 F.B. Gent published his *The Character of Sir Arthur Haselrig, the Church-thief*, in which he called Haselrig 'a day-bed for the devil', a 'villainous rogue' and 'a dissembler and liar'.

Haselrig became so powerful in Durham that locals began to refer to him as 'the Bishop of Durham', remembering the power the prince-bishops had once enjoyed in the area. Since his job had been abolished in 1646 the last bishop, Thomas Morton, had kept away from his old diocese, been banished from his house in London, and had even spent time in prison. Haselrig employed the disused cathedral as a prison, and bought the bishops' palace at Bishop Auckland as a grand residence for himself. For this he paid just over six thousand pounds; worth over six hundred thousand today. Recent excavations have confirmed that Haselrig used gunpowder to blow up the old chapel at Auckland Castle, and it is thought that he started to build a new house for himself somewhere on the site.

One source of both power and income for Haselrig was his involvement with the committees that were then charged with fining, and sequestering the property of, so-called 'delinquents'; people who had sided with or given aid to the Royalist side during the recent civil wars. The system might almost have been designed to encourage corruption, not least because the men who sat on the committees, like Haselrig himself, were able to buy properties they had seized, sometimes at a very attractive discount. The monies freed up by this process were supposed to go to pay the army and the other expenses of the new republican government. As a prominent Roundhead commander, Haselrig was liable to receive these monies direct, and in fact in the summer of 1646 the committee based at Goldsmith's Hall in London awarded Sir Arthur the equivalent of over seven hundred thousand pounds, in modern money, in recognition of his 'service to the Parliament'.

The republican government was suffering from a very lean purse, and had a great many expenses, including the maintenance of a large standing army. The process of extracting money from 'delinquents' of various kinds was often slow, and it seems that the work of a bullish man like Haselrig in this area was especially appreciated because he could cut corners, push things through and generally trample over legitimate opposition to his actions.

In order to find out who the Royalists were in a particular area, the committees relied on informants, who were rewarded with a percentage of the value of the property seized as a result of their revelations. For some tell-tales, this was an opportunity to settle old scores, impoverish or get rid of neighbours they'd never liked, or distract the authorities from their own 'delinquent' dealings with the Royalists.

Although he himself sat on committees charged with fining Royalist delinquents, John Lilburne's uncle George was plagued for years by just such an accusation, made in 1645 by a delinquent 'to smother his own guilt'. Back in 1642, George had been forced to sign warrants to supply horses to William Cavendish, the

Royalist first Earl of Newcastle. This was repeatedly used against George as 'proof' of his supposed Royalist sympathies, despite the sufferings he had undergone as a Parliamentarian in the northern counties when they were dominated by the Royalists.

George Lilburne was also involved in the next legal case his nephew John was brought into: it seems that this time John was able to combine family loyalty with legal work and his readiness to fight injustice wherever he found it.

The case concerned the coal-mines at Harraton in County Durham, mines that had been surrounded by complex legal controversies since at least 1599: this means that the case was even more long-running than the Axholme business in which John Lilburne had previously been engaged. The surviving papers relating to the Harraton controversy are full of contrasting opinions as to who owned the mines, who their rightful owner was and who should be put in charge; bearing in mind that the management of the mines themselves required a great deal of expertise and experience.

The mines at Harraton were finally closed, after centuries of coal production, in July 1964. By that time, they were no longer making a profit, but in the seventeenth century they were extremely productive and lucrative. In 1644 it was determined that the collieries were worth three thousand pounds a year, or over three hundred thousand at today's values. Like much of the coal mined in County Durham, the Harraton product was shipped out via the port of Sunderland. The Harraton colliery was so important that when it was inactive for a while due to a disastrous fire and a flood, the price of coal at Sunderland rose by around thirty percent.

For a time, the mines were controlled by a London leather-merchant with the unlikely name of Josiah Primate. Primate must have been a man of some wealth, because when the mines were flooded between 1642 and 1647, Primate paid nearly two thousand pounds to have them pumped out and made workable again.

Josiah did not run the collieries on a day-to-day basis: this was left to his tenants, two Georges: George Grey, and John Lilburne's uncle, George Lilburne.

In January 1652, Primate petitioned the House of Commons,

70

claiming that our old friend Sir Arthur Haselrig had wrongfully claimed the Harraton colliery for the Crown. Like Primate himself, Haselrig rented out the colliery, in his case to his military associates, Colonels Hacker, Mayers and Jackson, and a Major Tolhurst.

In his petition to the Commons, Primate claimed that members of Haselrig's committee had objected to Sir Arthur's swooping down on the Harraton colliery, but that when he, Primate, had appealed to the committee against their decision to hand Harraton to Sir Arthur, Haselrig himself had dominated the appeals procedure, 'and by his power and influence upon the committee he overawed most of them'. This was like a judge being allowed to sit on the bench to try a case in which he was personally interested. Winding up his petition, Primate begged for 'relief from the oppression and tyranny of the said Sir Arthur, and for the dispensation of justice'.

As in his Lincolnshire case, John Lilburne helped Primate's case by arranging for his petition to be printed, and by publishing his own account, called *A Just Reproof to Haberdashers Hall*, Haberdashers Hall being the headquarters of the London committee that was responsible for the Harraton case.

It cannot be said that the House of Commons' response to Josiah Primate's petition was what Primate would have wished for. Parliament upheld the original decisions of Haselrig and his committee, condemned Primate's petition as 'malicious and scandalous', and ordered it and Lilburne's *Just Reproof* to be burned by the common hangman. Primate was also fined a total of seven thousand pounds, and thrown into the Fleet prison. John Lilburne was fined the same amount, and forced into exile.

XI. Exile

John Lilburne was in exile on the Continent for some seventeen months. During that time, he drifted between Belgium, France, and the Netherlands. He may have reflected that his first serious brush with the law, back in 1638, had come about because of his highly suspicious visit to Holland. Now, in 1652, he had been forced to go to Holland as a punishment.

The English expatriate community, which at this time more or less revolved around the exiled court of King Charles II in Paris, included Royalists who had not yet come to terms with Cromwell's regime, and disappointed republicans and Parliamentarians who, like Lilburne, felt that the new republic was heading in an unfortunate direction. As Hester Chapman stated in her biography of George Villiers, one of the more prominent exiles, there were also the inevitable 'cheats, spies and cut-throats' among the bickering, embittered British abroad. An oddly-named fellow called Captain Wendy Oxford was certainly a spy, and cleverly attached himself to Lilburne on his passage over to Ostend. Lilburne quickly saw through him, suspecting that he would turn cut-throat and kill him if ordered to do so; but it was Captain Oxford who arranged the exile's first contact with Villiers, his most valuable friend on the Continent.

Many of the exiles had either lost or deliberately given up all or most of their incomes when they had opted to flee abroad, or decided that they were obliged to leave. Their lucrative estates back in England were now controlled by the republicans, and even the exiled king himself was notoriously hard-up. When Lilburne appeared in early 1652, his majesty and his followers were no doubt still smarting from their disastrous defeat at the Battle of Worcester in September 1651. This was the ignominious end to an ill-advised attempt by the Royalists to invade England from Scotland.

After the battle, Villiers, King Charles and others had had to slip over to the Continent in disguise, and when Dr Earle, Charles's old tutor, first came across him at Rouen, his highness was so shabby that the good doctor failed to recognise him, and even asked him where the king was.

At this time the king's mother, the diminutive French Catholic Queen Henrietta Maria, lived on a small allowance at the Louvre in Paris; but her means were so narrow that she was forced to tell her oldest son that himself and his followers could not even dine with her unless they paid for their own food. The widowed queen's followers formed one faction among the exiles – they were known as the Louvrains. Charles's own followers were divided among themselves: before his ill-fated Scottish adventure he had set up a government in exile at the Hague, made up of elder statesmen like the aforementioned Edward Hyde, Earl of Clarendon, and younger men like George Villiers. Clarendon in particular disliked and distrusted Villiers, regarding him as a bad influence on the young king.

It seems that when he turned up on the Continent in 1652, all sides regarded John Lilburne with suspicion. Was he a spy or *agent provocateur* working for his old friend Cromwell? Had he converted to the Royalist side, or was he ready to side with anyone who could get him back to England? Were his old ideas about the legal rights of the citizen still uppermost in his mind?

In an open letter to Cromwell, written after his return to England, and begging the Lord Protector for a pass so that he could stay in his homeland legally, Lilburne mentioned his extraordinary sufferings and the 'daily and hourly hazard of my life' that he had met with in exile; and indeed he narrowly escaped being murdered at Bruges when a group of drunken Cavaliers came to the house where he was living, only to find that he was out.

In exile, Lilburne continued to write as he had done in prison, and when he had been a free man, in his own country. He even bought a printing-press in Amsterdam to print his own writings, using thirty pounds he had earned with his pen. His works at this time were self-contradictory, and no doubt added to the confusion over what he was thinking, whose side he was on and what he was planning to do. In his *Apologetical Narration,* published in both English and Dutch, he advised Cromwell to set up a new parliament – this was still the era of the so-called Rump Parliament, which had been purged of members who disagreed with Cromwell. If Cromwell replaced this with something more democratic, Lilburne asserted, he would 'in the hearts of the honest and understanding people of England be esteemed really their darling'. In 1653, Oliver would dissolve the Rump altogether, declaring from the floor of the house, 'Depart, I say; and let us have done with you. In the name of God, go!'

As well as writing, Lilburne spent some of his time in exile catching up on his reading, taking in Machiavelli's *The Prince,* Walter Raleigh's *History of the World* and Plutarch's *Lives of the Noble Greeks and Romans.* He also read John Milton's prose work on the new English republic, the *Defence of the People of England.*

Cromwell's spies began to see Lilburne in exile as a serious threat after the Leveller was sought out by the aforementioned exiled Royalist, George Villiers, second duke of Buckingham. Buckingham had been at the disastrous Battle of Worcester with Charles II, and, while others applied for help to the Scots, the French or the Spanish, Buckingham at least entertained the idea that John Lilburne's enthusiastic supporters back home, stirred up by the Leveller's copious and inflammatory writings, might be able to overthrow Cromwell.

The unlikely friendship between Puritan John and Cavalier George shows how exile, like many other types of misery, 'acquaints a man with strange bedfellows'. Fourteen years younger than Lilburne, Buckingham was tall, handsome, blond, flamboyant, witty and reckless. He was the son of another George, the equally handsome but even more reckless favourite (and perhaps lover) of King James I, who had been a memorably incompetent Lord Admiral under Charles I.

As a teenager, Lilburne's new friend had run away from Trinity College, Cambridge to join Charles I's army and fight in the First Civil War. But the family had arranged for him and his twin brother Francis to go on a slightly early version of the Continental Grand Tour instead, taking in such places as Venice, Florence and Rome. The brothers signed up again when the Second Civil War broke out, and poor Francis was killed in action near Kingston upon Thames in 1648.

Hester Chapman wonders at how two such different men as Lilburne and Villiers could have communicated at all in a meaningful way, but it may be that the author of *Great Villiers* forgot about John Lilburne's pretensions to gentility, his repeated insistence on his high birth and good education, and the way that, against all the odds, he always managed to look well-dressed, at least for his portraits. While assuring Buckingham that Cromwell was 'as false a perfidious rogue as any in the world' and that he, Lilburne, 'had once as great a power as he has, and greater too, and am as good a gentleman, and of as good a family', John might also have been thinking that there was no reason why he, one of the Durham Lilburnes, should not be friends with the Duke of Buckingham.

Despite their differences of background, education, outlook and personality, Lilburne was also able to write very warmly about his new young friend in his *Defensive Declaration* (1653):

his powerful influence among the desperate Cavaliers being such that . . . he principally preserved my life from the many complotted designs . . . cunningly laid . . . to get me murdered

Lilburne and Buckingham met for the first time at Amsterdam, and according to, among others, Sir Edward Nicholas, a prominent member of the exiled royal court, Lilburne intrigued Buckingham with his ideas for the overthrow of Cromwell. As Sir Edward wrote in a letter from Amsterdam, Lilburne claimed that he could restore Charles II to his kingdom if:

he [Charles] will put all his forts, castles and ships, and likewise the militia of England, into the hands of the people of England, and be constantly governed by parliaments in all affairs that concern the commonwealth of England

If the king would agree to those terms (which sound a lot like the system of constitutional monarchy now in place in the United Kingdom) Lilburne claimed that he could raise forty thousand men for the Royalist side. Unfortunately the Leveller stipulated that he would also need ten thousand pounds to overthrow Cromwell; equivalent to over a million today, and far beyond King Charles's means at that time.

Hester Chapman presents this scheme of Lilburne's as something he really did propose to Buckingham: M.A. Gibb has her doubts, believing that the Leveller was not so treacherous as to plot against his own countrymen. Gibb insists that he later swore that he had not plotted in this way, but Pauline Gregg suggests that his oaths on this subject may have been equivocal. Gregg also suggests that, as usual, Lilburne talked too much and got carried away with his own words. Deep down, did he really believe he had forty thousand men who would rise at his command?

Despite the consolations of literature and intrigue, Lilburne found exile hard, but although she did not have to look over her shoulder for assassins at every moment, John's wife Elizabeth also had a wretched time while the sea divided them. She had a miscarriage, and in their father's absence she was entirely responsible for their children, who were often in bad health. As well as the expense of supporting the family, she now had to scrape together money for trips to the Continent. Frequently desperate and distraught, she was forced to sell or pawn her furniture and other possessions, and to sell a share in a house in London for considerably less than it was worth.

Elizabeth also had to sit on committees with her husband's enemy Sir Arthur Haselrig, in the hopes that she and her husband would get what was due to them from a property in County Durham that had been assigned to them. Worst of all, perhaps,

Elizabeth's relationship with John was beginning to break down. He said that she was 'filled with womanish passion and anger', and resented her failure to support any new attempts by him to write controversial tracts.

XII. The Old Bailey

Although the country and its new military dictator Oliver Cromwell had treated him as badly as they dared, Lilburne, like Buckingham, missed England and was desperate to return home. He took Cromwell's dissolution of the Rump Parliament in April 1653 as a sign that better days were to come: in this, he was seriously mistaken. Oliver did not call new, free and fair elections, but set up a nominated assembly of members hand-picked by the army for their religious rectitude. This group became known as the 'Barebones Parliament' after one of its members, a preacher called Praise-God Barebone who, like Lilburne's old client Josiah Primate, was also a London leather-merchant.

Lilburne reasoned that since his banishment had taken place under a parliament that no longer existed, he was now free to return home. He knew that he would probably need a special pass, but for some reason he seems to have thought that with Cromwell in a new and uniquely powerful position, the granting of this pass would be a mere formality. He was wrong again. By late May 1653 he was waiting at Calais ready for the good news that never came. Cromwell was determined not to send any pass that would allow Lilburne to return to England legally, although John had written to Oliver promising that his good behaviour would be guaranteed by a number of respectable London citizens, including William Walwyn, and his father-in-law, Henry Dewell.

Now determined to return home even without an official pass, Lilburne enjoyed a farewell supper with Buckingham at the Silver

Lion inn at Calais, then boarded a ship for Dover. From there he travelled to Canterbury, where his wife had fresh horses waiting for him. Told to produce his pass in the Lord General's name, Lilburne declared that he was as good a man as Cromwell, and needed no pass. Soon he was in London.

Now at home, John Lilburne was entirely at Cromwell's mercy. It was from his lodgings at Moorfields that he wrote his *Banished Man's Suit for Protection*, in which he told Oliver about his 'extraordinary' sufferings in exile, where he was 'in such daily and hourly hazard' of his life. The *Banished Man's Suit* was written after Lilburne's friend William Kiffin, and John's wife Elizabeth, had waited to see Cromwell for several hours, but without success. The text shows that Lilburne was now painfully aware of the 'provocations' he had 'put upon' Cromwell in his recent writings. He hopes:

that the harshest and most disgustful passages in them might possibly be construed to be the fruits of my highest passions, when my reason was clouded, not only by my sad and most heavy sufferings, but also by the misapprehensions of your excellency's actions and intentions, which I could not have the knowledge of beyond the seas, but as others misrepresented them unto me; hereupon I hoped that God in his mercy to me, and my poor ruined family, might incline your mind so to conceive of all former passages of whatsoever nature

This seems like a big ask, especially when it is followed up by broad hints about Cromwell calling a new parliament sooner rather than later. If he read the *Banished Man's Suit* at all, it seems that Cromwell was not convinced by Lilburne's new-found humility: the next day, John was seized and thrown into Newgate. Buckingham's enemy, the Royalist chronicler Clarendon, wrote that 'Lilburne appeared undaunted, and with the confidence of a man who was to play a prize before the people for their own liberty'.

Although the Rump, which had banished Lilburne, had been dissolved by Cromwell, the Act of Parliament by which John had been banished had never been repealed, and so in theory Lilburne's new trial at the Old Bailey should have been a routine affair. All the court had to do was prove that Lilburne had returned to England illegally. If the authorities had hoped that this could be brought off quickly and quietly, they were mistaken. Once again, the whole of England seemed to rally behind Lilburne, even before his trial began.

It was reported that twenty eminent Londoners stepped forward to offer bail for John, at twenty thousand pounds apiece. One of the new newspapers of the time reported that 'it cannot be expressed what posting here is up and down about John Lilburne in city, country and army'. Petitions and deputations were cropping up everywhere, and the aforementioned MP Praise-God Barebone was confronted by Katherine Chidley, a leading Leveller, with eleven other women, trying to present a petition supporting Lilburne, containing some six thousand women's signatures. Barebone found himself buckling under their arguments, but another MP was sent to assure them that 'they being women and many of them wives . . . the law took no notice of them'.

This time, Lilburne was tried at the Old Bailey, which then stood adjacent to Newgate Prison (which was demolished, after seven hundred years of service, in 1902). This was the medieval Old Bailey courthouse, which burned down in the Great Fire of 1666, and was re-built in 1673. Despite the new location, Lilburne's 1653 trial unfolded much as his Guildhall trial of 1649 had done, with the prisoner using every available tactic to put his prosecutors off their stride and take control of proceedings. As in 1649, the court-room was packed with Lilburne's supporters; his father was present, as was his father-in-law and the Leveller Samuel Chidley, son of the Katherine Chidley who had presented her petition to Parliament's representative, Praise-God Barebone. Lilburne's supporters did not hesitate to applaud everything their hero said or did in court, as if he were a much-loved actor, singer, or dancer.

The popularity of Lilburne's last trial as an event may in part be accounted for by the fact that in Puritan London during the Interregnum many forms of public entertainment had been suppressed. The theatres, which had hosted the premières of plays by Shakespeare, Marlowe and Jonson had been closed since the outbreak of civil war in 1642, and in London in 1656 Colonel Thomas Pride himself, who had supervised the purging of Parliament in 1648, ordered the death by shooting of all the bears used in the grisly spectacle of bear-baiting. Shakespeare himself knew the entertainment value of a well-written courtroom scene, especially one where the prisoner is innocent and pleads fearlessly for his or her cause. Such scenes can be read in Shakespeare's *Henry VIII*, where Catherine of Aragon is startlingly outspoken at the bar, and *The Winter's Tale*, where the innocent Hermione pleads for her life and appears to faint away and die in court.

Although his judges included the Lord Mayor of London, the Recorder, and the Attorney-General, Lilburne refused to be over-awed by them. In fact he tried to make some of their statements seem absurd and contradictory: when Prideaux, the Attorney-General, tried to get him to admit to being the very John Lilburne named in the Act, Lilburne insisted that he had no right to act as a judge, and suggested that the court 'thrust him down to the bar . . . and know his office and duty'. When the clerk of the court suggested that Lilburne should be gagged, he accused his accusers of trying to murder him 'without right of law' and characterised 'all your proceedings against me, from first to last' as 'a malicious packed conspiracy'.

Outside the court-room, the streets were thronged with well-wishers, and many both inside and outside the court complex were armed. In case things got ugly (which they certainly could have done if Lilburne had been sentenced to be hanged) three whole regiments of horse were posted nearby, ready to wade in.

Since May of the previous year the Venetian Lorenzo Paulucci had been in London, watching the progress of the new British republic. He reported to his masters that Lilburne himself had claimed that, if he was executed, twenty thousand men would avenge his death. According to Paulucci, Lilburne, 'with a courage exalted both by warfare and by literature' added 'other expressions' to this prophecy 'which have caused great anxiety to the Council of State'. Others said that the day of John's execution, if it ever happened, would prove to be the bloodiest day that

London had ever seen.

At one point during the trial, the court became so chaotic that a guard of horse was sent in to restore order. Lilburne refused to continue until they were removed, which soon happened. Although the various tricks John employed to reduce the court to chaos certainly played their part, his defence case was based on a good legal foundation. Not only had the parliament that had drawn up the Act by which he had been banished been dissolved; by banishing him it had acted as a law-court in itself which, Lilburne maintained, it had no right to do. It had proved a lousy law-court in any case, since it had banished Lilburne without indicting him, or summoning him to plead his side of the case. Further, there were inconsistencies between the Act itself and the judgement passed down to Lilburne. John also argued that there was no firm proof that he personally was the John Lilburne named in the Act. As in 1649, Lilburne stood at the bar with his copy of Coke's *Institutions*, and read aloud from this book to illustrate his legal points.

According to Paulucci, Lilburne used 'close reasoning' in court to suggest that if laws made by the recently-dissolved Rump Parliament were upheld (even though that parliament had been thrown out 'for injustice, irregularity and maladministration') then Oliver had surely been wrong to dissolve the Rump, and 'punishment ought first of all to be inflicted on Cromwell as the principal author of its unjust dissolution'. The Venetian characterised this argument of Lilburne's as a way for him to cast shade on 'his chief enemy'.

During the Old Bailey proceedings, an attempt was also made by John's prosecutors to throw shade on the prisoner by bringing up accusations that he had worked with and for the Royalists during his exile. The accusations contained in a printed pamphlet with a title beginning *Several Informations and Examinations Taken Concerning Lieutenant-Colonel John Lilburne* made little impact in court. In typical style, Lilburne countered *Several Informations* with another pamphlet called *Malice Detected*, swore that the claims were untrue, and wrote that they were 'a poisonous ingredient that his adversaries have always in readiness to cast into his dish'.

Paulucci wrote that:

Cromwell's power together with the proofs of the turbulent and seditious character of Lilburne might lead to a capital sentence did not the actual state of affairs require caution, as such a spark might kindle a great conflagration. So it is probable he will undergo severe imprisonment, instead of the death penalty.

The Venetian's prediction proved to be accurate. After listening to a speech of some two hours from Lilburne, his jury found him 'not guilty of any crime worthy of death'.

XIII. Jersey

Despite the widespread belief that the authorities could not execute Lilburne because of his continued popularity, it seems that Oliver Cromwell for one had been hoping for a guilty verdict. Clarendon tells us that, when he heard about Lilburne's not guilty verdict, the Lord General responded as he was wont to do after the loss of a battle. Paulucci reported that the outcome of Lilburne's latest trial caused Cromwell 'extraordinary annoyance' because he had 'anticipated a contrary verdict'.

By contrast, many Londoners rejoiced at the trial's outcome. There were cries of 'Long live Lilburne', and even the soldiers deployed in large numbers to deal with any disorder blew their trumpets, shouted and beat their drums.

Though technically his Old Bailey jury had found him not guilty, evidently there was never any question of setting the Leveller leader free. Under cover of night, he was quietly transferred to the Tower of London, and the Council of State took the shocking step of interrogating the members of the jury who had acquitted him. Still inspired, perhaps, by Lilburne's rousing speeches in court, the jury members whose answers under questioning have survived seem to have showed themselves to be resistant to the over-awing power of the intimidating Council.

The foreman of the jury, a local tallow-chandler called Thomas Greene, refused to explain his decision to the Council, stating merely that 'he did discharge his conscience in what he then did'. A book-binder called Richard Tomlins also played it close to his chest, but did offer his opinion that the John Lilburne who had been put on trial that summer was not the same man who had been banished by the Rump; otherwise, said Tomlins, 'he was not obliged to give any account of what he did'.

Other jurymen remained convinced of what Lilburne had told them, drawing on his copy of Coke; that they as jurymen were not only judges of the facts, but of the law itself. Legally, this was quite wrong, and is still not the case today in English courts, but Lilburne himself asserted it during many of his dealings with the law. If it were the case today in English court-rooms, the judges' role in advising the jury about the laws relevant to the case at hand would in fact be irrelevant, and the jury would presumably spend some of their time in the jury-room wading through legal tomes, trying to make out which laws applied, and how to apply them.

Lilburne was kept in close confinement in the Tower, but even under these conditions he was seen as a threat to the *status quo*, at least in London. There was a strong possibility that the law of *habeus corpus* might allow him to go free: in February 1654 one Captain Streeter, imprisoned by the Council of State for publishing seditious pamphlets, was released on a writ of *habeus corpus*. Fearing that Lilburne might try the same route to freedom, the Council dispatched the prisoner to the Channel Island of Jersey in March 1654. Pauline Gregg stated that *habeus corpus* did not apply on Jersey, but in his 2019 book *Law, Liberty and the Constitution*, Harry Potter argues that, though the island had a different constitutional status to much of mainland Great Britain, in theory there was no reason why a writ of *habeus corpus* could not have effect there.

Although orders such as the one to transfer Lilburne to Jersey may have come from the Council of State, for the rest of Lilburne's life his fate was entirely in the hands of one man: Oliver Cromwell. This was not a good situation for Lilburne: Cromwell had good reason to resent him, suspect him, even fear him and the Leveller group he had once led. As Gibb suggests, the Protector was far too busy at this time, keeping himself safe from assassination and trying to steady the ship of state, to want to have to deal with more challenges from a restless, outspoken malcontent.

The fact that Cromwell had put himself in a position where he could ride roughshod over the law in this way now made him a symbol of the kind of thing the Levellers did not want to see in England. When it came to Lilburne, Oliver could not even try to win his gratitude by releasing him on the basis of a republican version of a royal pardon. From his cell on Jersey, John made it clear that he would not accept release unless it was on a proper legal basis. This, of course, might have involved the authorities having to admit that they had been wrong to smuggle him into the Tower after his last trial.

As Potter explains, in the seventeenth century the odd legal status of Jersey made it something like private land owned by the monarch, or even like the Bishopric of Durham in the days of the prince bishops – a discrete state within a state. In the Civil War, when Parliament objected to the gun-running activities of a leading islander, the Bailiff Sir Phillippe de Carteret, a powerful local figure, responded, quite rightly, that Jersey had nothing to do with Parliament but only with 'the king in council'. The Royalist gun-runner was the Bailiff's son George: George's father's defiance sparked a miniature civil war on the island. Sir Phillippe was forced to take refuge in Elizabeth Castle, while his wife sought the comfort of the castle of Mont St Orgueil. It was to this Norman fortress, which is also called Gorey Castle, that John Lilburne was sent as a prisoner in 1654.

In 1637 the Puritan William Prynne had been locked up in Mont Orgueil; he was not released until 1640. The Bailiff then, the aforementioned Phillippe de Carteret, had seen to it that Prynne was treated well; and the Puritan dedicated an edition of the verses he had written on Jersey to the Bailiff. This volume, which appeared in 1641, gives the impression that the solitude, the good treatment, good air and beautiful views Prynne encountered on the island delighted him and put him in a contemplative mood:

Shut up close prisoner in Mount Orgueil pile,
A lofty castle, within Jersey isle,
Remote from friends, near three years' space, where I
Had rocks, seas, gardens daily in mine eye,

Which I oft viewed with no small delight,
These pleasing objects did at last invite
Me, to contemplate in more solemn wise,
What useful meditations might arise
From each of them, my soul to warm, feast, cheer,
And unto God, Christ, Heaven mount more near.

As an unlikely friend of the Royalist de Carteret, Prynne wrote against de Carteret's enemy on Jersey, Michael Lemprière, who was Bailiff for the Parliamentary side during Lilburne's time at Mont Orgueil. It was Lemprière's attempt at a military coup that had forced de Carteret to resort to Elizabeth Castle. There the Royalist Bailiff died in the August of 1643, succumbing to an epidemic that swept through his garrison.

Though the 'rocks, seas, gardens' of Jersey seemed to suit Prynne, imprisonment on the island did not do Lilburne any good at all. His room was cold and, Potter suggests, he would have found it difficult to communicate with his native guards, since they spoke Jerriais, the Jersey version of Norman French. The Governor of Jersey, Captain George Gibbon, was ordered to keep Lilburne in close confinement, and to ignore any writ of *habeus corpus* that might appear.

Worse than the immediate circumstances of Lilburne's imprisonment was the fact that he could hear little news from home, and could no longer send out his habitual stream of pamphlets. At one point, he succeeded in getting a packet onto a ship heading for England, but the man who had it threw it overboard when it looked like he was about to be searched. Lilburne's only real company was an elderly woman called Elizabeth Crome, who seems to have combined the offices of nurse, companion and housekeeper. Lilburne later described her as 'moral, honest, careful and industrious' and 'really serviceable to me in my great distress in Jersey'.

It soon became clear that the regime of close confinement was having a deleterious effect on Lilburne's sanity, and so Gibbon arranged for his famous prisoner to exercise in the open air, in the castle precincts, as long as there was a guard with him at all times. The guard was not allowed to talk to Lilburne, and John refused to exercise in this way 'with a dog at his heels'.

Writing to Oliver Cromwell, Captain Gibbon complained about Lilburne's 'ill language and threatenings' and the 'many disorders' he caused. He added that Lilburne was 'more trouble than ten such as Ashburnham', referring to John Ashburnham, a leading Royalist and close companion of King Charles I, who was banished to Guernsey Castle three times during the republican period.

Perhaps because nobody had heard anything about him for a while, rumours began to circulate in London that Lilburne had died on Jersey. A pamphlet appeared, with the title *The Last Will and Testament of Lieutenant-Colonel John Lilburne*, and Paulucci reported that John had been 'put to death in prison without further trial'.

Lilburne was not dead, but the concern was that he would fret himself to death if he could not be talked into a calmer mood. From Cromwell's point of view, there was also the possibility that the restless prisoner would escape, organise an uprising of the castle garrison, or otherwise put himself into a position to challenge the government, either by writing pamphlets or planning a political coup. A revolution led by Lilburne, such as John had once told the Duke of Buckingham he could bring about, would no doubt have led to the execution of Cromwell. As Clarendon had said of John and Oliver, 'it is a measuring cast between them, and infallibly that one will hang the other'.

In June 1655 Cromwell sent Henry Dewell, Lilburne's father-in-law, to visit the exile on Jersey: Colonel Gibbon was instructed to report on how the meeting went, and on Lilburne's condition generally. Gibbon wrote that 'he is the very same man as formerly; I see no alteration' despite the efforts of 'the honest old gentleman, his father-in-law'. The governor went on to suggest that 'the likeliest way to bring his spirit to be meek and quiet' would be to put him 'in some garrison . . . nearer home, that some of his soberest and wisest friends might come to him and deal with him by arguments and persuasions one after the other'. Although Gibbon suggested the Isle of Wight, in October 1655 Lilburne was

moved to Dover Castle. There a new, wise and sober friend visited
him; Luke Howard, the Quaker shoemaker of Dover.

XIV. Luke Howard

John Lilburne was certainly aware of the Quakers as a group before he met Luke Howard in 1655: a Quaker associate called Henry Clarke had attended his trial at the Old Bailey. This Henry Clarke was the author of *A Description of the Prophets, Apostles and Ministers of Christ* (1655) and lived at Southwark. Lilburne had also read, and discussed with his friend William Harding, some Quaker literature while he was imprisoned on Jersey.

The Quakers, also called 'Friends' with a capital 'F', had been a startling and conspicuous presence on the British scene since 1652, when after years of neglect the teachings of a self-appointed itinerant preacher called George Fox began to 'convince' large numbers of people. (Although non-Quaker historians often use the word 'conversion' to describe the process of becoming a Quaker, 'convincement' is the correct Quaker term.)

George Fox was born at Fenny Drayton, a village in Leicestershire, in 1624. When he was barely twenty, he abandoned his apprenticeship to a shoemaker and took to the road, preaching a highly eccentric form of the Gospel. He suffered many privations and knew a great deal of inward suffering, but things began to go well for him and his Quixotic cause when he found allies among the members of a religious group called the Westmorland Seekers in 1652. Quakers generally count 1652 as the year of the true beginning of their Society, though Fox had been active as a preacher since 1644. Because of the historic role of the Westmorland Seekers, many Quakers refer to what the rest of the world knows as the English Lake District as the '1652 country'.

From the north-west, Quaker ideas spread so rapidly during the 1650s that some suspected that the Friends were witches, and were using some form of enchantment to convince their followers. There was, however, a great flourishing of diverse religious groups during the whole Civil War and Interregnum period. The Quakers had to compete not only with the Church of England, Roman Catholicism and the Presbyterians, but also with Baptists of various kinds, pseudo-religious groups like the Diggers, and also the Ranters, Muggletonians, Grindletonians, Fifth Monarchy Men and others. Of the groups that started up in those days, only the Quakers continue to have followers today: Baptists appeared on the scene earlier in the seventeenth century, when King James I was still on the throne.

The appeal of Quakerism, with its message of loving peace, must have been particularly appealing in the middle of the seventeenth century in England, when the country had been so battered by political upheaval and civil war. Many of the early Quakers had, like John Lilburne, seen action in the Civil Wars. Numbers were imprisoned for their religious beliefs, which were seen by the authorities as dangerously subversive. The original Quaker message was, however, deeply rooted in the Bible and traditional Christian faith, and for many early adherents their experience of convincement comprised a sharp reminder of what it meant to be a follower of Jesus.

Luke Howard, the Quaker shoemaker of Dover who helped convince John Lilburne, should not be confused with his better-known Quaker namesake, the nineteenth-century Quaker scientist. It was the later Luke Howard whose work on meteorology gave us the familiar names of the clouds that are still used today: cumulus, cirrus, etc.

The seventeenth-century Luke Howard, the Quaker shoemaker of Dover, was himself convinced after having first attached himself to several other religious groups in turn. These included the Presbyterians, the Independents, the Baptists, and even the Brownists, the last an early Puritan sect that originated in the sixteenth century. He also experimented with a more worldly way of life, 'and went to a draper and bought as much cloth as to make me four pair of breeches, and two doublets and a cloak, some very fine.' This is reminiscent of Lilburne's natty dressing, as seen in his engraved portraits.

Born at Dover and raised within the traditions of the Church of England, Luke might have followed his step-father's trade; that of butcher. Although vegetarianism was not much spoken of even among the most radical sects of the time, the future Quaker could not find it in his heart to don the butcher's bloody apron, and so took up the trade of his dead father: that of a shoemaker.

Like John Lilburne, Luke Howard was inspired by his master to take a closer look at the business of religion, while he was still serving his apprenticeship. In the short autobiography printed with other material in a book called *Love and Truth in Plainness Manifested* (1704) Luke explains how his master:

began to enquire after religion, and went amongst such as separated from the public worship, and began to make more conscience of religion than he had done; the which then opened a door to me

This is very similar to Lilburne's case: as we have seen, the future Leveller's master introduced him to radical political and religious thinkers, like John Bastwick, who were then in prison in London.

When he had served his apprenticeship, Luke Howard went to London where he joined an Independent congregation. He might have become yet another future Quaker who had fought in the civil wars, but his attempt to sign up as a Roundhead soldier was frustrated. His 'mind being earnest for the war' he:

took a horse at the Star on Fish Street Hill, with an intent to go into the army, and kept it ten days, but by reason of so many pressing to go and entering themselves, it fell to my lot (as the Lord ordered it) to be left out

At that time, he was 'troubled for my dismission of going into the war' but later rejoiced that this meant that he was 'clear of the blood of all men'.

Hearing that there were horses being offered to willing future army officers back home at Dover, Luke hurried there, only to find that the mounts had all been taken by the time he arrived. He then took up a post as a member of the garrison of Dover Castle, where John Lilburne would later be imprisoned, and where Luke himself would be imprisoned himself after the Restoration.

It may be that the young men of the Dover Castle garrison had too much time on their hands: in any case, they seem to have spent a lot of time brooding on religious matters or, as Luke himself put it, 'enquiring the way to Sion, and asking after it, with our faces thither-ward; and we gave up our minds to search the scriptures'. Luke found that during services held at the castle, he could no longer join in the singing of psalms, finding the practice 'a mocking service as to the Lord'. When a priest called Samuel Fisher was brought from Lidd in Kent to reason with him about this, Luke convinced Samuel that he too should too should 'sit silent in the Cross' when psalms were being sung. Later, Luke would decide that water-baptism was also 'but carnal' and irrelevant to real faith.

His doubts about the outward forms practised in the churches he had been attached to led Luke into a period of spiritual darkness, when he found himself 'in a waste howling wilderness, where I could find no trodden path, nor no man to lead me out of it, and into a way where I might find bread for my soul, and be refreshed'.

Luke Howard's first brush with Quakerism came in March 1655. He was in London on business and, perhaps looking for a guide who could lead him out of his howling spiritual wilderness, he attended Allhallows Church in Lombard Street to listen to the preaching of John Cordwell, a noted religious radical of the time. In his *Memoir*, Luke says nothing about Cordwell, except to say that he was 'a mystery-man so-called'. What the Kentishman did remember were the words of 'a young man, newly come out of the north-country', who stood up and spoke at the end of Cordwell's sermon. This was William Caton, a close associate and possibly a relation of Margaret Fell, of Swarthmore Hall in Cumbria, one of the most important early Quakers, who married George Fox himself in 1669.

That day in Lombard Street, Caton 'sounded an alarm out of Sion, and proclaimed the Gospel of peace out of the holy mountain', but, perhaps because he was a little hungry at the time, Luke was not impressed. He turned to his companion and said, 'I know as much as he can tell me, and more than I or he either can live in'. He then proposed to his friend that they leave Allhallows and go to dinner.

Luke Howard had made the error of mistaking the conventional Christian message of early Quakerism with commonplace preaching. He did not make the same mistake when he heard William Caton preaching again, in a church-yard in Dover a week or so later. Just the look of the young Friend now 'smote within me' and he made himself busy guarding Caton 'from the boys and rude spirits that offered him abuse'.

The 'rulers of the town' ordered the innkeeper where they were staying to eject William Caton and his companion John Stubbs. Luke Howard offered them shelter in his own house, and when the constables came to eject them, Luke refused to let them in. When the mayor complained that the shoemaker had disregarded a legal warrant for the arrest of Stubbs and Caton, Luke argued, in true John Lilburne style, that there could be no legal basis for such a warrant. 'They be my friends,' he declared; 'and what have you to do with them, any more than I have with your friends?'

There were Quaker religious meetings at Luke Howard's house, both before and after Caton and Stubbs, Luke's 'fathers in the truth' had continued on their missionary journey. The shoemaker began to adapt his whole way of life to the new Quaker way, dressing more plainly, refusing to take his hat off as a respectful greeting, and also refusing to use 'you' instead of the more familiar 'thee' and 'thou' in his conversation. Thanks to the shoemaker's efforts, Quakerism began to take root at Dover, or, as the Quakers themselves would say, 'the truth prospered'. But it was still a raw, enthusiastic Quaker with only a few months' experience of the Life who visited John Lilburne at Dover in the winter of 1655.

XV. Convincement

Shortly before his inauguration as eighteenth president of the United States in 1869, Ulysses S. Grant received a delegation of Quakers. Concerned that the Native Americans were not being treated justly, Grant asked the Friends to pick out 'Indian agents' from among their number. Such agents were sent by the Office of Indian Affairs to interact with the Native Americans in various settings. 'If you can make Quakers out of the Indians, it will take the fight out of them,' Grant suggested to the delegation, adding, 'let us have peace'.

One can imagine the members of the Quaker delegation shifting awkwardly from foot to foot in front of Grant, looking down at their feet, and at each other, in embarrassment. Surely we are not here to 'de-claw' the Indians, they might have said to themselves: we want to help them. Grant had not understood that Quakers *will* fight, but that their 'Peace Testimony', the official statement of their pacifism, formulated in 1660, makes it impossible for Friends to take part in 'all outward wars and strife and fighting with outward weapons'. The wording of the Peace Testimony implies that yes, there will be 'wars and strife', but that in such conflicts, Quakers will turn to weapons other than the sword, the gun, the missile and the land-mine.

If, pre-empting Grant's idea, Oliver Cromwell had managed to recruit a tame Quaker to de-claw John Lilburne, he would have been falling into the same misunderstanding that Grant fell into. As a Quaker who had promised never to take up a gun or a sword again, Oliver's old enemy could still have been a very dangerous opponent of the Protector and his military dictatorship. As a born-again pacifist, Lilburne might have been particularly effective as a critic of the Protector's disastrously warlike foreign policy; dragging up such matters as his siege of Drogheda in Ireland 1649. Notoriously, Drogheda turned into an indiscriminate massacre after the Roundheads broke into the town.

An important source for Lilburne's convincement is his intriguingly titled 1655 pamphlet *The Resurrection of John Lilburne*. Like Luke Howard, for Lilburne the process of his transformation out of his old ways into the new ways of the Friends was not in itself peaceful. There was no sense of Free-born John relaxing into a warm bath of pacifism and brotherly love. Like Luke, Lilburne suffered intense spiritual anguish. In a letter to his wife Elizabeth printed in *The Resurrection* he states that the 'carnal', 'fallen' man he used to be is being 'crucified by the will and wisdom of Jesus' and that Jesus has also brought him 'shame of soul'. Later in the letter, Lilburne describes the 'real fight' he has fought; something akin to what the Catholic mystic St John of the Cross called 'The Dark Night of the Soul':

the real fight (in its measure and degree) and spiritual consideration of these things, since I last saw thee, for diverse hours in several nights, one after another, when my God denied sleep unto my outward eyes, and caused my soul to be awake with himself and to be really exercised in an interchange of divine conference, contemplation or parley with him, has even caused my soul to weep, sigh, and mourn within me

Even without such inner strife, Quakerism in the middle of the seventeenth century in Britain could never be considered an easy option. Friends were still mercilessly persecuted in those days.

Lilburne's own account of his first brush with Quaker ideas includes more language relating to violence than we might expect from a story about a man embracing a new, peaceable world-view. *The Resurrection of John Lilburne* includes a letter to his friend William Harding, who was then mayor of the town of Weymouth on the Dorset coast. In the letter, Lilburne admits that when he had finally come to terms with two substantial Quaker books in his cell in Jersey Castle, he was 'knocked down off, or from my former legs, or standing' and forced to reject many of his former ideas and 'my old bustling ways in the flesh'. As well as being 'knocked down', Lilburne felt that his old 'wit, wisdom and desires' had been 'struck down dead to the very earth', as Saint Paul had been on the way to Damascus, 'fallen down flat at the feet of Jesus'. In much the same way, the Dover shoemaker Luke Howard repeatedly used the word 'smote' in relation to his slightly earlier convincement.

As well as being 'knocked down' and 'struck down' just by reading Quaker literature on Jersey, Lilburne admitted that a key exchange with Luke Howard in his new prison, Dover Castle, left him speechless. One source for this can be found among extracts from the old records of the Quakers of Kent, printed in a book called *The First Publishers of Truth* (ed. Norman Penney, 1907).

Probably while discussing some religious or political issue of the day, John asked his visitor, 'I pray, sir, of what opinion are you?' Luke answered simply, 'None'. This answer left the once loquacious Leveller at a loss for words. Emerging from his profound silence he at last asked meekly, 'What must I say, and how must I speak?' Luke Howard replied, 'Thou mayest speak what is in thy own mind, and after thy own manner.'

'You say, you are of no opinion,' Lilburne went on.

'I do say so,' Howard confirmed, 'for really I am of no opinion.' At that, the conversation stalled for the second time; but Lilburne asked Luke Howard to visit him again.

Of course Luke Howard had no *opinions* – he had reached the stage in his spiritual journey where what he had instead were *convictions*. But when John Lilburne was allowed to walk into Dover itself to attend a Quaker Meeting for Worship, he experienced a similar sensation to that felt by Luke Howard when he first heard William Caton preach in London: he liked the preaching of a Quaker called George Harrison, but found that 'his wisdom was above it'. Here we may be seeing the old Lilburne pride asserting itself again. Harrison was no doubt preaching in simple language, and not introducing anything into his message that could not easily be found in an English New Testament. He was using language that was as plain as the Friends themselves were supposed to be in their habits and appearance. But John Lilburne, with his minor gentry background and reasonable level of provincial education, may have found it all a little too plain. As he left, Harrison himself ran after him and cried out, 'Friend, thou art too high for truth'. These words gave Lilburne a stunning 'box on the ear'.

Lilburne had been caught out by one of the characteristic paradoxes of the Christian faith. The best Christians recognise that, in the eyes of God, many people who may seem of absolutely no consequence in the human world are very highly regarded in Heaven, and can look forward to a fine old time when their souls pass into eternity. From the Christian point of view, the last come first, and the story of St Paul's experience on the road to Damascus, as related in the New Testament Book of Acts, includes details of how the saint's 'Damascene moment' left him blind and helpless. By the time he came to write the texts that comprise his *Resurrection* pamphlet, Lilburne had come to terms with this and had no qualms about how 'contemptible' the Dover Quakers had seemed to him at first.

Reading Quaker literature, Lilburne developed a particular admiration for the writings of James Nayler, whom he describes as 'that strong, or tall man in Christ'. Nayler's life was similar to Lilburne's in many respects, and their personalities shared features in common. Both could inspire great loyalty, affection and even love in many people, especially women, yet both were also reckless and liable to find themselves at the centres of great controversies.

James was only four years younger than John. They had both served in the Parliamentary army, Nayler as a quartermaster; possibly a regimental quartermaster. While Lilburne repeatedly got himself into trouble through his writings, Nayler shocked both Quakers and non-Quakers when he rode into the city of Bristol, attended by his adoring followers, in a way that reminded everyone of Jesus' entry into Jerusalem on the first Palm Sunday. This happened about a year after John Lilburne's first contact with Dover Friends. Nayler was arrested, tried for blasphemy by

Parliament itself and sentenced to a punishment similar to, but much worse than, that suffered by Lilburne in 1639.

James Nayler was not only tied to the back of a cart and whipped as he was walked through the London streets: after he had been fixed in the pillory he was also bored through the tongue with a hot poker, and branded with a capital 'B' on his forehead, since he was regarded as a blasphemer. It is likely that Nayler's whipping was more severe than Lilburne's had been: witnesses reported that there was not a scrap of skin left between his neck and his hips.

Given his injuries and subsequent imprisonment it is astonishing that Nayler managed to live for another four years. He died in 1660, a few months after the Restoration of King Charles II, in a year that John Lilburne would never see. Nayler's punishment was surely made worse by the fact that for a time many Quakers, including George Fox, disowned him. This resembles the way that many of Lilburne's erstwhile supporters distanced themselves from him after his exile to Jersey. Few came to visit, and those who did seemed to be more concerned with Lilburne's mental state than with restoring him to his former status as Leveller leader and England's agitator-in-chief.

The words James Nayler uttered on his death-bed comprise perhaps the most beautiful statement of the Quaker idea that has yet been made. Here, he reminds us of the central role of humility in Christianity as the Quakers understood it, and mentions how the crown offered by the Holy Spirit is 'meekness'. This crown can only be kept by 'lowliness of mind'. The spirit also brings 'fellowship . . . with them who lived in dens and desolate places in the earth'.

It is lazy to characterise John Lilburne's Quaker convincement as the story of a man's sudden switch from the political to the religious sphere. For Lilburne, it was always about religion: indeed, in his writings he was in the habit of finding scriptural justifications for ideas relating to the English constitution which would have been completely alien to the original authors of the books of the Bible.

A strong sense that Lilburne's activism was religiously inspired can be felt in his own account of his 'censure' in London in 1649. In *A Work of the Beast* he tells us that when a young man offered him a few words of encouragement just before his punishment commenced, he replied:

> . . . I am cheerful and merry in the Lord, and am as well contented with this my present portion as if I were to receive my present liberty. For I know my God that hath gone along with me hitherto, will carry me though to the end. And for the affliction itself, though it be the punishment inflicted upon rogues. yet I esteem it not the least disgrace, but the greatest honour that can be done unto me, that the Lord counts me worthy to suffer anything for his great name.

Lilburne's words to his young friend in 1649 show a preparedness to suffer for the truth – something Quakers were forced to do throughout the early years of the Society. Many, including George Fox himself, were harassed, beaten up and left to rot in prison, both in Britain and in her colonies, and hundreds died as a result. Their experiences were recorded in Quaker 'books of sufferings', which now serve as invaluable sources for historians of the early growth of Quakerism. The necessity of supporting Friends trapped in prison had a lasting effect on the structure of the Quaker hierarchy, at least in Britain. One of the most important national Quaker bodies is still called the Meeting for Sufferings. Although, even in his broken condition, John Lilburne may have been willing to suffer for his new faith, he was spared that in his last few years.

While Quakerism was taking Dover and other places on the south coast of England by storm, the missionary work of George Fox and a dozen others was making major inroads in Lilburne's home county of Durham. One of them, John Audland, wrote that 'the harvest here is great' and that he could 'really see the Lord will raise up to himself a pure and large people to serve and worship him in spirit and in truth'.

XVI. Silence

Lilburne's new faith brought him a new inner contentment, but it did not bring him permanent freedom from imprisonment at Dover Castle, and it certainly did not solve the practical problems that still dogged himself and his family. These included a serious lack of cash, exacerbated by the monumental fine of seven thousand pounds that was still payable. Most of the suffering associated with their poverty fell on the shoulders of Elizabeth Lilburne. In the letter to his wife that is printed in *The Resurrection of John Lilburne*, John regrets that she is 'so straitly put to it for money' but suggests that, if only she could share his faith, the family could live happily together without any money at all. He asserts that his wife would then be 'pleasant in mine eyes' though 'clothed in rags' and suggests that she should try to 'live upon God by faith in the depths of straits'.

In a man without responsibilities, deliberately embracing a life of pious poverty might seem praiseworthy, but it seems unfair of Lilburne to expect Elizabeth and their children to simultaneously raise their religious game and be happy that they were poor and hungry. In any case, John did continue to work with Elizabeth to try to regain his right to the income from his Durham property, though his ability to do so was severely hampered by the fact that, though he was often allowed out on parole, he was still a prisoner.

As had been the case for some time, one obstacle to Lilburne regaining his Durham rights was the powerful figure of Sir Arthur Haselrig. While he still had his foot firmly placed on the neck of the Lilburnes' hopes, one of his associates was making life in general for the Quakers of Durham much easier than it was in other parts of England. Anthony Pearson, Haselrig's secretary, a local judge and an important man throughout much of the North, had become a Quaker after an encounter with the aforementioned James Nayler. In 1653, Nayler was tried for blasphemy at Appleby, as he would be later in London, by Parliament itself. At Appleby, he spoke so inspiringly in his own defence that Pearson, one of his judges, was convinced.

Pearson was based at Ramshaw Hall in County Durham, a fine house that is still standing, though it is much altered since Anthony's time. Like Haselrig himself, Pearson sat on committees charged with dividing up property belonging to 'delinquents', and had acquired property for himself in the process.

It was probably thanks to Pearson's influence that a compilation of the sufferings of the early Quakers published by Joseph Besse in 1753 included only one paragraph relating to Durham before 1660. The paragraph in question mentions the cases of three men whose property had been seized because of their refusal to pay tithes; something the Quakers generally refused to do. As a Quaker, Anthony Pearson was very active in defending Friends' right not to pay tithes, a tax from which, in theory, the established church was supposed to benefit. In the same paragraph in Besse's *Sufferings* we learn about Margaret Ramsey, imprisoned for preaching after the priest's sermon in church, and George Humble, locked up for objecting to a judge who had had his friends put in the stocks. Described by Besse as 'an honest old man', Humble died in prison after ten months' confinement.

When Anthony Pearson, acting for Haselrig, returned some of the property Lilburne claimed was his, John was incensed because the way the transaction had been conducted implied that Haselrig had a legitimate claim to all the property, and was merely giving some of it away as a charitable act. Once again, Lilburne was standing up for rights, though this time it was not for the rights of all the people, but for his own rights in relation to certain pieces of property.

Frustrated by Haselrig's continued control over what he regarded as his by right, Lilburne now turned to his new Quaker friends for assistance. He talked to Luke Howard, John Stubbs and one John Higgins, also a Quaker, at Dover, and obtained leave to go to London to consult with more Friends in the capital. In London, he talked to Henry Clarke, the Quaker he had known before he had been convinced himself. Lilburne lodged at Woolwich, where he was visited by John Slee, a Cumberland Quaker. Slee agreed to convey papers relating to Lilburne's case to the aforementioned Margaret Fell, mistress of Swarthmore Hall in Cumbria, which was then serving as a headquarters for Quakerism in the North-West.

It is likely that Margaret and her husband Thomas could have helped Lilburne: Thomas Fell was a powerful figure locally, a judge and Member of Parliament with a great deal of legal experience and expertise. Margaret, known as 'the mother of Quakerism', was a born organiser who helped establish, among other things, a practical system whereby Quaker work could be funded.

Unfortunately Lilburne's final effort to claim his legal rights was not to bear fruit during his lifetime, despite the cooperation of influential Quaker friends. The Leveller died on the twenty-ninth of August 1657, at Eltham in Kent, during a visit to his wife. Elizabeth had just given birth to another child, perhaps their tenth, and she was 'lying in'. In those days (and for many years afterwards) women who had just given birth were advised to 'lie in', in other words keep to their beds for a time, partly because it was believed that if they did not do so, their wombs would become deformed.

Eltham, once the site of a medieval royal palace mentioned by the poet Chaucer, is nearly seventy miles from Dover: Lilburne was able to be there thanks to an extended period of parole. He died on the day he should have returned to Dover Castle. In her biography of the Leveller, Pauline Gregg makes much of the fact that Eltham is only a few miles from Greenwich, where earlier Lilburnes had mixed in royal circles.

It is not clear what Lilburne actually died of. It was certainly not old age: he was probably only forty-three at the time. In her 1947 biography, Gibb blames 'years of privation, of struggle, and of endurance'. It may be that the slow onset of the disease that killed him sapped his restless energy over several months and made him more liable to listen to the still small voices of the early Quakers.

John Lilburne's body was brought to the then headquarters of the Quakers in London, the Bull and Mouth inn in Aldersgate. Some say that the inn's name was a corruption of 'Boulogne Mouth' where King Henry VIII had won a famous victory in 1544, at which time Bartholomew Lilburne, one of John's forbears, may have been in attendance.

In the seventeenth century, it was the custom to honour the dead by putting a fine cloth or pall over the coffin for the journey to burial, much as flags are sometimes draped over the coffins of the military dead today. The plain Quakers did not approve of this, and so Lilburne's coffin was taken out into the street uncovered. There an unidentified man tried to throw a costly velvet pall over it, but this was removed. John Lilburne, gentleman, Leveller, Quaker, was buried in a new churchyard near the famous Bethlehem Hospital. According to Gibb, this was on the site of what is now Liverpool Street.

Elizabeth was now left to look after herself and her children on next to nothing, with a fine of seven thousand pounds still unpaid. Oliver Cromwell responded to her plea for help, allowing her to be paid the pension of two pounds a week that John had received during his last imprisonment. This was the equivalent of over two hundred pounds today; and Elizabeth later admitted that this meagre income saved her and her children from death by starvation.

Cromwell survived John Lilburne by little over a year, dying in September 1658. During the short reign of his son and successor Richard Cromwell, Parliament decided that the Act that had led to John Lilburne's fine and imprisonment had been illegal, and it was repealed in August 1659. As a result, the fine of seven thousand pounds vanished as if in a puff of smoke. The pension of two pounds a week continued to be paid to Elizabeth and her children.

Less than a year after the Act that had condemned John Lilburne had been abolished, Charles II returned to England as king, landing at Dover on the twenty-fifth of May 1660. This Restoration must have caused some consternation among the Durham Lilburnes, who cannot have forgotten that John's older brother Robert had been one of the so-called 'regicides', who had signed the death warrant of Charles I. The new King Charles would have had every right to have had all thirty-nine of the surviving regicides executed: by 1660, twenty of the original fifty-nine signatories were dead. Robert lilburne was tried and sentenced to be hanged, drawn and quartered, the most grisly form of execution imaginable, but his sentence was commuted: he was imprisoned on Drake's Island in Plymouth Sound, where he died in 1665.

John Lilburne's aristocratic friend Gearge Villiers, second duke of Buckingham, claimed to have returned to England in disguise several times before the Restoration, but these claims may only have been tall tales. He did return in 1657, the year of Lilburne's death. He was imprisoned, and then released thanks to his powerful friends. Although he was greeted coldly by Charles II on his return, he was soon in favour again, gained many high offices and was soon being called the richest man in the country.

Although he was not a regicide, at the Restoration Sir Arthur Haselrig was imprisoned in the Tower of London, where he died in 1661. Persecution of the Quakers continued after 1660, and one of the victims was Luke Howard, the shoemaker of Dover. Luke endured two periods of imprisonment at Dover Castle, where he had once been a member of the garrison, and further time in prison at Canterbury. Anthony Pearson, the Durham man who had done so much good for the Quakers, particularly in his home county, renounced his Quakerism and re-joined the Church of England. He died in 1670.

The Restoration of King Charles meant the restoration of the bishops, and John Cosin, the first bishop of Durham after the Restoration, busied himself with reclaiming every scrap of property that had been snatched from the diocese while the bishops had been abolished. Like many in the new Royalist establishment, Cosin was also an enthusiastic persecutor of the Quakers; although he employed a local Quaker builder to put up his almshouse, which still stands on Palace Green in Durham City.

Cosin's builder, John Longstaff of Bishop Auckland, was one of the long list of County Durham Quakers arrested in 1660 and imprisoned for refusing to take the Oath of Allegiance and Supremacy. Whatever the wording of the oath, Quakers could not take it because they believed that no oaths should ever be taken by a true Christian. It is hard to argue with this position, since Jesus himself forbade the taking of oaths (see Matthew 5:34).

Besse reports that the new Quaker prisoners in Durham Gaol 'met with a very avaricious inhuman gaoler' who demanded two shillings and sixpence a week from each of them, to pay for their beds. When the Friends refused to pay this, the gaoler threw twenty of them into a tiny cell, so small that they could not all lie down at once. At the end of his account of Quaker sufferings in Durham in 1660, Besse mentions four Friends who were heavily fined for 'absence from the national worship', i.e., failure to attend Church of England services.

XVII. Lilburne Right or Wrong

It is likely that if the legal rights and freedoms John Lilburne had campaigned for throughout much of his adult life had been firmly enshrined in law in the 1650s, much of the persecution of the Quakers that continued after the Restoration would have been legally and constitutionally impossible. The Leveller leader would no doubt be delighted to hear that in Britain today the law itself can effectively prevent and, if necessary, undo damage caused by the agents of the law themselves. At times the law can even roll back the effect of illegal actions carried out by the government. In September 2019, for instance, Prime Minister Boris Johnson attempted to prorogue (or 'suspend') Parliament in a way that seemed arbitrary to some, and reminded others of similar attempts by King Charles I and Oliver Cromwell. After two weeks, the Supreme Court ruled that the prorogation was unlawful, having the same effect in law as a blank sheet of paper. Parliament resumed sitting straight away.

In *Great Villiers*, her biography of the unlikely friend John Lilburne made during his Continental exile, Hestor Chapman suggested that the 'plans and ideals' of Lilburne's Levellers have now been 'realised by democracies all over the world, having first been put into practice by the creators of the United States of America'. The fact that U.S. Supreme Court Chief Justice Earl Warren mentioned John Lilburne in his writings about the famous case of Ernesto Miranda suggests that at least one American remembered the early struggles for citizen's rights, in another part of the English-speaking world.

In her book, Chapman reflects on how the spirit of the Levellers' 'schemes' and 'prescriptions for erring and unfortunate humanity' were now 'adopted in all civilised countries'; but adds that Lilburne and his group were so far ahead of their own time that few of their contemporaries could have believed that the rights and freedoms that they advocated could one day be established in law. Actions such as the attempted prorogation of the U.K. Parliament in September 2019 are reminders that such rights should never taken for granted.

Chapman has to admit that the Levellers 'enjoyed a very moderate success' in their own time 'and are now, as a group, almost forgotten'. Understanding of them is further frustrated by the misleading label 'Leveller', and the tendency to confuse them with the True Levellers or Diggers whose aims were quite different. Given the obvious justice and value of the Levellers' ideas, can we attribute their comparative failure as a movement to the restless, abrasive character of their leader?

Although Hester Chapman, Judge Earl Warren and many others have shown their admiration for what John Lilburne tried to do, the Victorian writer Thomas Carlyle took violent exception to the Leveller's character. In an 1848 letter to Thomas Wise, in which he discussed the idea of writing a biography of Lilburne, Carlyle insisted that the long period of research required would not be worth the candle if the result was a study of this 'contentious, disloyal, commonplace man, little distinguished save by his ill nature, his blindness to superior worth, and the dark internal fermentation of his own poor angry limited mind'. In the same letter, Carlyle goes on to call Lilburne a man of 'poor capabilities' and 'that Puritan Thersites'.

The name 'Thersites', applied by Carlyle to Lilburne, will seem particularly harsh to any reader familiar with Homer's *Iliad* or Shakespeare's *Troilus and Cressida*. Shakespeare inherited Thersites from Homer – he is a revolting, foul-mouthed malcontent, and an embarrassing critic of those in authority over him. As Alexander Pope's translation of Homer's *Iliad* has it, Thersites is:

Loquacious, loud and turbulent of tongue:
Awed by no shame, by no respect controlled,
In scandal busy, in reproaches bold:
With witty malice studious to defame,
Scorn all his joy, and laughter all his aim

In his letter to Wise, Carlyle not only resists the idea of writing a biography of Lilburne because he dislikes him – he also complains that there was very little useful information about the man available in the middle of the nineteenth century. For Carlyle, Clarendon offers 'various anecdotes and details; which are to be regarded mostly as mere rumours, and false, or unworthy of belief without better proof': otherwise researchers will soon find themselves sifting through what Carlyle calls the '50,000 unread pamphlets' known to Carlyle as the King's Pamphlets, but to modern researchers as the Thomason Tracts.

In his letter, Carlyle suggests that given the availability of sources, and the qualities of the men in question, a new biography of the Quaker leader George Fox might offer 'the basis of a really useful, honourable and important labour in the field of English history', especially since, Carlyle claims, Fox's life was 'utterly dark' to readers in the middle of the nineteenth century. The author of *Sartor Resartus* implies that, by contrast, a biography of Lilburne would be unworthy of the 'loving labour' required to write it, and unlikely to appeal to any publisher. For him, Free-born John was not 'an apt hero for a *Life and Times*'. Luckily for twenty-first century readers, a number of authors and publishers since Carlyle's time have felt that both Fox and Lilburne were worthy of extensive biographies.

Carlyle's rejection of Lilburne as a worthy subject for biography must be viewed in the context of his book *On Heroes, Hero-Worship, and the Heroic in History*, based on a series of lectures delivered by the Scotsman in 1840. In the first lecture, Carlyle asserts that 'the history of what man has accomplished in this world, is at bottom the History of the Great Men who have worked here'. It is important, he implies, for others to recognise the qualities of these Great Men (always written with capitals by

Carlyle), to try not to hinder their great creative work, or to stand in the way of their bright light (they are living 'light-fountains', according to Carlyle).

Carlyle includes among his Great Men (there are no Great Women) the pagan god Odin, the prophet Muhammad, Dante, Shakespeare, Luther, John Knox and, in the last lecture, Oliver Cromwell (Carlyle would later edit an edition of Cromwell's letters and speeches). It may be that by what he calls Lilburne's 'blindness to superior worth' Carlyle meant the Leveller's determination to block and frustrate the Lord Protector. This suggests that Carlyle had indeed found the sources on Lilburne available to him inadequate, or had not read them properly.

The Leveller's relationship with Cromwell was so emotional, and went through so many changes, that a whole play, film or novel could be based around just that. As we have seen, Lilburne, whom Carlyle criticises for 'his blindness to superior worth' was actually employed by Cromwell to report on the worth or otherwise of his superior officers during the First Civil War. At times, as we have seen, Lilburne expressed tender affection for and gratitude to Cromwell; and when his criticisms of Oliver did not come from raw anger and frustration, they were similar to what many others were saying, both nationally and internationally, about the Protector. Cromwell had, after all, invited criticism by allowing a republican revolution to turn into a military dictatorship. He had also frustrated democracy and, having helped to overturn the monarchy, had made himself into something very close to a monarch.

Apart from Cromwell, who were the other people of 'superior worth' to whose fine qualities Lilburne was wilfully blind? The rapacious Arthur Haselrig? The judges who kept Lilburne in prison, although a jury of his peers had acquitted him? The officials who tried to intimidate that jury after they had made their judgement?

In the bitter words of Carlyle's letter to Wise, the Scotsman mentions 'the dark internal fermentation of [Lilburne's] own poor angry limited mind' . As well as piling up far too many adjectives, the phrase seems to be an ill-advised attempt to psycho-analyse the

Leveller leader, and to guess at what we would now call his 'motivation'. Lilburne may indeed have had dark internal fermentations, which would have been entirely natural for a man unjustly locked up in prison, or sent into exile because he had been brave enough to get between Parliament and some of its income. But at this distance in time, it seems rash to speculate on the mental sources of Lilburne's actions. What matters is that he stated time and again in his writings that he was trying to defend what he saw as the just laws of England, to protect the rights of the individual, and to act in a way consistent with the dictates of Christianity.

Even if we suspect the motivation of this man; who could indeed be angry, bitter and vengeful at times, we should also bear in mind the lasting effect of the best of what he did: he spoke truth to power, and sometimes managed to frustrate the arbitrary and oppressive actions of the powerful. Sometimes, when the authorities triumphed over him, Lilburne's public profile and his widely-read utterances exposed the corruption of those in charge and turned their triumphs into pyrrhic victories.

If we judge Lilburne's words and actions by their effects, we must, however, admit that in some areas their effects were unfortunate, to say the least. His enviable ability to make friends was matched by a strong tendency to alienate the very same friends, sometimes with disastrous results. In his relationship with the powerful figure of Oliver Cromwell, this hot and cold approach to friendship caused him great suffering, and probably shortened his life. Some say that the Levellers were, in effect, the first English political party. Because of his tendency to make enemies, Lilburne as leader of the Levellers seems to have anticipated the style of some modern party leaders, who tend to fragment, rather than unite, their parties.

It may be that Lilburne's tendency to cast off valuable allies came from a key quality of Lilburne's that Carlyle does not mention in his letter to Wise: his restlessness. This it was that seems to have made it impossible for him to settle into the various professions he tried his hand at when he was not actually in prison. We are told that what were in effect guild restrictions made it impossible for him to build on his apprenticeship as a clothier and live and die in that profession, but he also had the chance to grow fat and comfortable as a military officer, government official, a brewer, a soap-boiler and an amateur lawyer. The law business might have worked better for him if he had not chosen the vexed Harraton case, which set him against the government's agents, or if he had not fought that case as if it were another moral crusade, complete with ill-advised pamphlets.

Behind Lilburne's unsuccessful and perhaps half-hearted attempts to earn a living by trade may have lurked what we might call his suspicion that as a son of the land-owning gentry he should not have had to work at all, and should have been able to live comfortably on a private income. Thanks in part to the actions of Arthur Haselrig, Lilburne was never able to set up such an arrangement to his satisfaction during his life-time, but his determination to try to do so led to some unfortunate consequences. Pauline Gibb goes into some detail about a family called Huntingdon who were tenants on a farm Lilburne laid claim to. Lilburne himself was quite open about wanting them off his land, though eviction would have meant considerable hardship for them. Eventually they were evicted by force, and John's father Richard took possession of the farm.

If Lilburne's restlessness tended to fragment his followers, render the Levellers' efforts fitful and unfocused, and make it impossible for him to stick at a profession, it also had a deleterious effect on his wife and children. For far too long, Elizabeth Lilburne found herself the wife of a convict, forced to work hard not only to bring up their offspring but also to petition for her husband's freedom, or some alleviation of the conditions under which he was held. She also had to work to secure their income and property, and was forced to journey to Durham to see what she could do in the Huntingdon case mentioned above.

John Lilburne was certainly not always appreciative of his wife's superhuman efforts, and he showed his resentment of her just complaints more than once in ways that were entirely inexcusable. Although modern Quakers might find *The Resurrection of John Lilburne* a beautiful affirmation of the joys of

Quaker convincement, it could not have been comfortable reading for Elizabeth. Here was her husband, having assimilated the new, plain language of an embattled sect, publicly implying that she should be more pious, and even embrace a worse level of poverty. Of course Elizabeth was soon having to convince the authorities in London that her husband's convincement was genuine, and that he and his new Quaker friends were not hatching political plots behind a smokescreen of peaceful piety.

As Hester Chapman implied, John Lilburne was a man ahead of his time: a campaigner for the rights of the individual in a place and time when those in power, whether royal or republican, simply would not allow those rights to be upheld. Lilburne was also a man of his *own* time in that, in a way that can seem eccentric to the modern reader, he often couched his utterances, on such matters as the right to a fair trial, in profoundly religious language. Some claim that Lilburne was in some ways *behind* his own times in that his background made him the product of a world that was already beginning to pass away. In the seventeenth century, the small-scale town and city craftsmen of England, with their protective trade organisations, were a medieval anachronism. The small landowners were starting to look anachronistic as well: as any of the Durham Lilburnes could have told their famous relative, it was becoming tough to make a decent income from land; much better to invest in mines, or the commerce of a city like Sunderland.

Whether he was an anachronism or very much a product of his own turbulent times, John Lilburne is still relevant today. Although the battles he fought have been won in some countries, his ideas would still seem radical and advanced in others. Even in countries where civil rights are enshrined in law, they are not always upheld at the level of individual court-cases, or the preceding interactions between, for instance, suspects and officers of the law.

The 1948 United Nations Universal Declaration of Human Rights contains thirty articles, many of which, such as the right to a fair trial with legal representation, address issues close to Lilburne's heart. John would also have approved of the right to own property (Article 17) and, as a member of an Independent church who turned Quaker, the rights to freedom of religion, and also to change religion (18). Lilburne might never have thought of some of the other rights in the Universal Declaration, but the degree to which these rights are neglected even in England in the twenty-first century is a reminder that battles such as those fought by John Lilburne still need to be fought.

How many people in England today even know that, under the Declaration, they have a *right* to employment, a fair salary, paid holidays and reasonable working hours? How many in the United States appreciate that they have a *right* to healthcare, and support in old age? How many refugees arriving on the shores of Europe understand that they have a *right* to claim protection?

Select Bibliography

Ackroyd, Peter: *Civil War*, Pan, 2015

Archer, Mark: *A Sketch of the History of the Coal Trade of Northumberland and Durham*, King, Sell & Railton, 1897

Besse, Joseph: *A Collection of Sufferings of the People Called Quakers*, Luke Hinde, 1753

Braddick, Michael: *The Common Freedom of the People*, Oxford, 2018

Braithwaite, William C.: *The Beginnings of Quakerism*, William Sessions, 1981

Brockie, William: *Sunderland Notables*, Hills, 1894

Carlyle, Thomas: *Selected Writings*, Penguin, 2015

Chapman, Hester: *Great Villiers*, Secker & Warburg, 1949

Chapman, Hester: *The Tragedy of Charles II in the Years 1630-1660*, Cedric Chivers, 1964

Chernow, Ron: *Grant*, Head of Zeus, 2017

Clair, Colin: *A History of Printing in Britain*, Cassell, 1965

Clarendon (Edward Hyde, First Earl of Clarendon): *The History of the Rebellion*, Oxford, 1843

Como, David R.: *Blown by the Spirit*, Stanford U.P., 2004

Dodds, G.L.: *A History of Sunderland*, Albion, 2011

Firth, Charles: *Oliver Cromwell and the Rule of the Puritans in England*, Putnam's, 1900

Foxley, Rachel: *The Levellers*, Manchester University Press, 2013

Gibb, M.A.: *John Lilburne the Leveller*, Lindsay Drummond, 1947

Gregg, Pauline: *Free-Born John*, Harrap, 1961

Hill, Christopher: *The World Turned Upside-Down*, Penguin, 1975

Hind, Albert L.: *History of Fatfield and Harraton*, 1974

Huens, G. (ed.): *Selections from Clarendon*, Oxford, 1955

Marcombe, David (ed.): *The Last Principality*, University of Nottingham Press, 1987

Meikle, Maureen: *Sunderland and its Origins*, Phillimore, 2007

Records of the Committees for Compounding, etc. With Delinquent Royalists in Durham and Northumberland, Surtees Society, 1905

Moore, Rosemary: *Light In Their Consciences*, Penn State Press, 2010

Pope, Alexander (trans.) *The Iliad of Homer*, Henry Frowde, 1903

Richley, Matthew: *History and Characteristics of Bishop Auckland*, W.J. Cummins, 1872

Rutherford, Ward: *Jersey*, David & Charles, 1976

Smiles, Samuel: *Lives of the Engineers*, John Murray, 1904

Stonehouse, W.R.: *The History and Topography of the Isle of Axholme*, Longman, 1839

Surtees, Conyers: *History of New Shildon and East Thickley*, 1923

Webb, Simon: *The Dunbar Martyrs*, Langley Press, 2017

Webb, Simon: *The Life and Times of John Duck*, Langley Press, 2019

Wilson, Charles: *Holland and Britain*, Collins, 1950

Short Titles of Works by John Lilburne Cited in the Text (in date order)

1638 A Work of the Beast

1641 The Christian Man's Trial

1645 A Copy of a Letter . . . to Mr William Prynne

1645 England's Birthright Justified

1645 Innocency and Truth Justified

1646 The Freeman's Freedom Vindicated

1646 The Just Man's Justification

1649 The Second Part of England's New Chains

1649 Legal Fundamental Liberties of the People of England Revived

1651 A Just Reproof to Haberdashers Hall

1652 Apologetical Narration

For free downloads and more books from the Langley Press,
please visit our website at http://tinyurl.com/lpdirect